Praise for *Wo*

As I read this book, I felt like I was reading about "special forces experts" in the steel and manufacturing industries. Lund interviewed women in steel, steel-related and manufacturing industries around the world. No matter where the interviewee lived or where she worked, there are stories of strength, knowledge, commitment, passion, challenges, solutions, and vulnerability while answers were being sought to find and maintain a place at the table. This is a strong message for those industries that are having difficulty finding and keeping a qualified workforce and demonstrates the value and insight women as leaders are bringing to these industries.

– Autumn Edmiston,
CEO, Edmiston Group

Some of my best and early career mentors and advocates were woman in the steel industry. One I worked for, one I worked with, and one I still do business with after almost 40 years. They are knowledgeable, passionate, and some of the strongest negotiators I have had the pleasure of dealing with. I am glad to see a book dedicated to showcasing amazing women from around the world and their journeys in this industry.

– Al Thomas,
Director Supply Chain,
Gibraltar-SEMCO

WOMEN IN STEEL WOMEN OF STEEL

WOMEN
IN STEEL
WOMEN
OF STEEL

Yesterday, Today & Tomorrow

Volume I

Karin J. Lund

Women In Steel, Women Of Steel
Yesterday, Today & Tomorrow

ISBN: 978-1-949955-06-4 (paperback)
ISBN: 978-1-949955-07-1 (eBook)

For permission requests, contact the author at

KJLund@G-PowerGlobal.com or www.G-PowerGlobalPublishing.com, or visit www.G-PowerGlobal.com

Cover Design by Christy Day, Constellation Book Services, www.constellationbookservices.com

Photographs supplied by the interviewees

The content of this book is for general consideration only and intended to provide helpful information concerning the subject matter covered. It is not an attempt to be an exhaustive reference for all the subjects listed in the book. This book is sold with the understanding that the author and publisher are not engaging in any kind of medical or psychological relationship with the reader, and the reading of this book does not imply such. The reader of this book should not rely on the information in this book as a substitute for medical or psychological advice from a physician, psychologist, psychiatrist, or another licensed health care provider. The author is not responsible for any health needs before, during,

Printed in the United States of America

Dedication

This book is dedicated to the women who have committed their careers and lives, past and present, to the steel industry and steel-related businesses.

And to the women in the future who will become the new leaders in this industry, we embrace you.

> "Do not go where the path may lead,
> go instead where there is no path
> and leave a trail."
> – *Ralph Waldo Emerson*

Contents

Introduction   1

Chapter One   Dr. Ruth *Is* in the House   5
Ruth Engel
Refractory Consulting Services
Owner

Chapter Two   A Warrior's Heart   21
Barbara R. Smith
Commercial Metals Company
Chairman, President and CEO

Chaper Three   A Grandfather's Vision and a Matriarch's Legacy Live On   49
Anna Mareschi Danieli
Danieli Group
Vice Chairwoman Steelmaking Division

Chapter Four   "I am going to be a CEO by the age of 40."   67
Carol R. Jackson
HarbisonWalker International, Inc
Chairman of the Board, President and Chief Executive Officer

Chapter Five   She Stands on the Shoulders of Her Great-grandmother   91
Roxanne Brown
United Steel Workers Union, Washington DC
International Vice President At-Large

Chapter Six   A Five-Year Business Plan at the Age of Twelve!   105
Eva Dillon
ArcelorMittal Dofasco
Steelmaking Technology Business Unit Manager

Chapter Seven	Here Comes the Judge!	133
	Elena Petráškova'	
	U.S. Steel Košice	
	Vice President, Subsidiaries and General Counsel	

Chapter Eight	"I don't really keep a notch on the belt for the wins." I take a stripe on my back for the losses."	151
	Shaina Huntington	
	TMS International	
	Manager, Marketing & Engineering	

Chapter Nine	Stories from a Steel Trader— "You have to know how to work the deal."	169
	Catherine Walsh	
	Steel Trader	

Chapter Ten	"I don't have a problem stepping up if I need to and I don't have a problem stepping back if I need to."	189
	Kelly Dallas	
	Cleveland-Cliffs Inc.	
	Director of Engineering-Flat Rolled	

Chapter Eleven	"Stand By Your Can"and "Captain Steel"	203
	Jennifer Wylie Faines	
	PR Digital Communications	
	CEO	

Chapter Twelve	"Never underestimate the power of a hot dog."	221
	Sara Dadig	
	Buyer	

| Acknowledgments | | 227 |
| About the Author | | 231 |

Introduction

A friend had asked me to attend a Pittsburgh chapter dinner meeting for the Association for Iron & Steel Technology (AIST) in January 2019. As I was talking to the gentleman sitting beside me at dinner, I heard my name called twice by the emcee. I walked up to the front of the banquet room and learned I had won a year's membership in AIST. That dinner began a three-year journey and a reconnection to the steel industry through AIST—a connection I thought I had severed forever.

I received information about the AISTech Convention to be held in Pittsburgh in May 2019 and noticed a session called *Women in Steel Roundtable* in the schedule of events. I asked a longtime member of AIST to join me at this session where we were seated with another "steel veteran" in the industry. As we discussed our careers, we realized that between the three of us we had 113 years of experience in the industry.

I listened as the attendees introduced themselves and briefly described their positions at their respective companies. It struck me that women would not have been considered for many of these positions when I first started in the industry.

I realized how women's roles in the industry had evolved. It was at this meeting that I began to formulate the idea of capturing these women's stories and their experiences in the steel industry over a fifty-year time span—a living history, so to speak.

I envisioned a book that would include women who had been in the industry their entire careers, women who were relatively new in the industry, and everyone in-between. Through their stories it was my goal to create an awareness about the variety of career opportunities that are available in the steel industry.

In addition, by reading about the challenges and successes of these leaders in executive and management positions, it would provide women with the opportunity to visualize themselves becoming successful in these various roles.

Since attracting and informing people about the industry is a global challenge, I wanted this book to go beyond North America and include interviews with women in the steel industry from other countries.

I approached Stacy Varmecky, general manager of sales and marketing, for AIST, and asked for her thoughts about the project. She agreed to speak to a newly formed steering committee at AIST, which was assessing barriers to entry for women in the industry, and the committee agreed to support the project.

AIST sent out a blanket inquiry to female members in AIST from around the world asking if they would like to be interviewed as part of the project. Within twenty-four hours after the initial inquiry was emailed, I had twenty-six positive replies. To date, I have interviewed more than sixty women in the industry, which equates to 120 hours of interview conversations.

This is my third book, and I have come to the respect that books develop a rhythm and style all their own. This book is no different. I was somewhat surprised but very pleased with the three main themes that emerged from my interviews. The first is that job progression is seldom linear, and this certainly has been the case in the successful career paths of the women who were interviewed for this book. Choices and saying "yes" to new opportunities and sometimes unique challenges afforded beneficial experiences that led to new management positions for each of the women I interviewed.

Secondly, the interviewees openly discussed ideas, shared their thoughts, and hard-won wisdom and management styles, lessons that will hopefully serve to educate, inspire, and motivate readers in their own personal career paths.

The third theme allows readers to sense the genuine passion the interviewees have for the steel industry, and their respective companies, whether they have been in the business for three years or thirty. Through the stories of these dynamic women, readers can view a traditional industry from new perspectives, particularly the idea that steel is a technology-driven industry with an abundance of exciting career opportunities.

Lastly, by sharing these collective experiences I want to encourage the industry to understand how they can become more inclusive and provide more positive role models that encourage women to join and grow within the industry.

Look for the second volume of *Women In Steel, Women Of Steel, Yesterday, Today & Tomorrow* in May 2023.

Karin J. Lund

CHAPTER ONE

Ruth Engel

Refractory Consulting Services
Owner

Dr. Ruth *Is* in the House

In 1970, a seventeen-year-old girl in Santiago, Chile, stood before the American embassy's vice consul. Salvador Allende had been elected as president of Chile and there was a great deal of political fallout and upheaval in response to the election worldwide.

Following the election, this native Chilean was determined to return to the United States, finish her senior year in high school, and attend college. Ruth had been a foreign exchange student in the Youth for Understanding program and lived with her host family in Grand Rapids, Michigan. The family was anxious to welcome her back. The bond they had formed was strong, and she would remain close to them for the rest of their lives.

When Ruth applied for a three-month tourist visa back to the United States, the vice consul accused her of wanting to stay in the States longer than the visa

Ruth, age 16, in Chile

allowed. They argued back and forth, and the vice consul finally said, "The United States does not want people like you coming into the country."

Even so, Ruth received her tourist visa. She flew to the United States, graduated from high school, and was accepted to the University of Michigan in Ann Arbor, where she earned both a bachelor's and master's degree in geology.

Ruth had always been interested in geology. If she had stayed in Chile, assuming she was accepted into the geology program, she would have had another challenge to overcome. In order to receive your college degree in Chile, you had to complete an internship in your field. The only internships related to geology were in the petroleum fields and the mines, and neither field accepted women.

I think of a brave teenage girl, amid political chaos in her native country, making the decision to leave her country, family, and friends. How many of us at seventeen would have the emotional maturity to make that decision? A decision that would ultimately affect the rest of her life. It would be her single-mindedness and the strength of her convictions that would define Ruth's choices and career in the steel industry.

Ruth met her husband of forty-eight years while she was in college. They married and he accepted a teaching position at Miami University in Oxford, Ohio. On their way to Oxford, she remembers seeing the Armco Steel mill in Middletown, Ohio, which is now owned by Cleveland-Cliffs.

As you can imagine, southern Ohio did not offer a plethora of opportunities in geology. Ruth had always been interested in material sciences, so she applied for a research position at Armco with the refractories and graphite group. At the time, Armco was the sole international representative of Lincoln Electric products outside the United States. Lincoln was a major welding products and equipment company, headquartered in Cleveland, Ohio. The project Ruth was hired for was the reverse engineering of welding fluxes. She was also responsible for providing technical support to Lincoln's overseas manufacturing facilities.

Ruth was only the second professional woman to be hired at Armco. When she started working at the research center there were approximately two hundred people employed at that location.

How were you accepted in the group?

The research group had interviewed numerous candidates but voted unanimously to hire Ruth. She had to prove herself as anyone does who is new in a position and young.

* * *

The group that Ruth worked with included seven professionals; two were hired to work on welding products and everyone else worked on refractories and graphite electrodes. On Friday afternoons, the group would meet to discuss their successes, challenges, and trials. Years later, Ruth recognized how much she'd learned during those Friday sessions. She enjoyed the open discussions about the problems the group faced. She watched and listened to how they helped one another create solutions and strategize. It was a great training background for her—an experience for which she is eternally grateful.

Her boss became a mentor and would help her prepare for the Friday afternoon meetings and when they visited steel plants. Debates were often heated, loud, and aggressive. Every line item of data was scrutinized in relation to a problem or challenge. You had to be prepared to defend your position on every issue, trial, improvement, or failure. Before each meeting, her boss would challenge Ruth's ideas, thoughts, and suggestions. He did so based on knowing how everyone would react to her positions. She learned how to be thorough with her analysis and would come prepared, having already debated both sides of an argument or suggestion. She became so proficient in these discussions that eventually her antagonists stopped questioning her assumptions and accepted her analysis. She admits she missed those group challenges and discussions. In her mind it was another way to further quantify her findings.

In R&D work, individuals would develop and submit product and send it to the lab for testing. If the product satisfied the needed properties, a trial was sent to the customer for field testing. Ruth was responsible for developing formulations and manufacturing product for the welding program. Since it can take weeks or months for feedback from these tests, Ruth began working on refractory projects in the steel mills to fill in the time gaps. Eventually, she moved into refractories full-time after the welding program was discontinued. During this time, she worked hard to educate herself and expand her knowledge about how steel was produced. She also attended seminars on the topic.

Eventually, Armco eliminated the refractory research group and Ruth was one of only two people left. She was assigned projects to improve the quality of steel.

Within six months, the mills realized they needed help in the refractory area and reached out to Ruth. She asked top management to authorize the request and spent about 50 percent of her time on refractory failure analysis and the other 50 percent on steelmaking issues.

Armco became AK Steel. In time, the company underwent a major staff reduction and Ruth was fired. She says, "Being fired is a badge of honor in the steel industry."

Ruth started in the industry on January 1, 1979, and left AK Steel in November 2003, just shy of twenty-five years. Although she was fired, she continued to work with AK Steel on and off for thirteen years.

During the Iron and Steel Society days, before the Iron & Steel Society (ISS) and American Iron & Steel Engineers (AISE) merged to become the Association for Iron & Steel Technology (AIST), Ruth served on the board of the electric furnace division.

In 2006, Ruth formed her own company, Refractory Consulting Services, and specializes in failure analysis, insurance work, and refractory training.

In 2021, the American Ceramic Society presented Ruth with the Theodore J. Planje St. Louis Refractories Award, otherwise known as the Planje Award, for: "Distinguished achievement in the field of refractories."

She received two awards at AISTech in Nashville in 2021. The first award was the Benjamin F. Fairless Award for: "A lifetime of contributions to the steel industry; and for her tireless and enthusiastic dedication to the support of steelmakers, the Iron and Steel Society and AIST, and to educate the next generation of refractory specialists in understanding the importance of refractories and their use."

The second award she received was the Distinguished Member and Fellow Award: "For exceptional tenacity in maintaining the industry's focus on the importance of, and dependence upon, refractories within the steel production process routes; for her valuable contributions to improving these steelmaking processes; and for her service as a dedicated committee member and educator for 35 years. Engel is an outstanding role model and mentor for women engineers around the world."

Congratulations! Dr. Ruth, as she is known, was certainly "*in* the house" at AISTech 2021 in Nashville.

Ruth Engel receiving Distinguished Member and Fellow Award from 2019-2021 AIST President Ronald Omalley.
(Photo courtesy of AIST archives)

What were several of your biggest challenges throughout your career?

Early in her career, the challenge was to be accepted as an equal and taken seriously. Being the only female never bothered her. "You rarely noticed you were the only female in the room. It seemed everyone else was there to notice it for you."

Another challenge was getting over the feeling that she knew less than what she did. She never studied refractories/ceramics or engineering, but acquired her knowledge through attending short courses, conducting her own research, and through hands-on experience. For her: "Crawling through godforsaken places in the mills never bothered me. If you are willing to spend the time getting dirty, the guys generally respected you, and if you are doing a trial at the mill, you better be there, even if it is three in the morning."

Did you have any challenges when you were pregnant and had to go out into the mill?

She felt that everyone was rather protective of her. While some may think that was patronizing, she didn't look at it that way. "If everybody watches out for every-one else, it is that much safer."

How did you and your family handle traveling for business?

She quoted something that her eleven-year-old daugh-ter said to her: "I like that you did not make me part of your project."

11

For a time, she was flying to Pittsburgh or Baltimore at least every other week and sometimes weekly. The staff at the car rental places and hotels had cars ready for her, and hotel staff greeted her by name.

Did you have any issues with any of the men when you visited the mills?

She had one incident with a manager she was working with. He had approved a trial and thought he deserved "a special favor." After that comment, Ruth had no further conversation with him, nor did she ever return to his office. She never reported the comment or incident to anyone.

What has been most gratifying in your career?

She said that if people at the company were in a meeting and discussing a refractory trial, they would run it by her. If she agreed with the trial or would suggest any changes, or process improvements, there was inevitably an acknowledgment from someone that "she knew her stuff." That recognition meant a lot to her.

Ruth has been in the field for decades. She is confident and knowledgeable in many different industries. About eight years ago, Ruth was involved in a legal case. She represented a company that was suing a refractory installer. The female attorney she was working with, who was much younger than Ruth, said: "Thank you for paving the path for me and others."

What is your definition of success?

"To be recognized within the steel industry, to be knowledgeable in the area you work in, and to be able to handle or deal with new challenges. Not only is it important to be technically knowledgeable, it is important to teach, and to teach the next generation. Once you have a certain knowledge base, and you have attained certain insights, you should pass this knowledge to the next generation."

What is your definition of mentoring and have you done any mentoring?

She has mentored students, and her definition of mentoring is to be there to answer questions. She feels students should "have a very solid theoretical background, and a theoretical background will allow you to work in many areas."

What is your definition of failure?

"Never really finding something that you enjoyed doing. If you feel you are stuck, try to find something you enjoy. No matter what you do, and as much as you might love it, there will be weeks, or months, where you are absolutely miserable. Doing something that you love will allow you to look forward to the future."

What is your definition of happiness?

"To be satisfied with what you're doing, whatever that means to you personally. It is different for every person. It's different for whatever circumstances you live in, and what stage in life you are in."

From a young age, Ruth was never dissuaded from asking questions. She would ask questions and people would answer. When she was in high school in the United States, a teacher encouraged her to ask questions. The teacher was lecturing on a book they had read and used the word "BS." She didn't know what "BS" meant, so she raised her hand and asked. Everyone, including the teacher, laughed and he explained what "BS" meant. After that, she never hesitated asking questions.

What interests you about this book?

Ruth likes the idea of this book because it highlights the variety of jobs that go into making a ton of steel.

What have you learned about yourself during your career?

She feels it was important to speak up. She believes it was important to thank people and think about what you say before you say it. She feels it is always better to write your thoughts down before you speak and has had some feedback that she is more effective when she writes versus when she speaks. She also believes you need to learn how to work with people and not steamroll them.

Do you have any regrets?

She regrets not spending more time in the mills early in her career. However, she qualifies that comment by saying that if she had spent more time in the mills, she wouldn't have benefited from those Friday afternoon technical meetings with the research group. What she learned in those meetings became a fundamental aspect of her success in the industry. In those meetings she learned how to identify, articulate, propose, and defend suggestions and ideas for addressing a process, a problem, or a new opportunity.

✻ ✻ ✻

Based on her experience in the industry, Ruth advises, "I would like for people of any age to see and imagine yourself in many different ways. It doesn't make a difference if you are a woman or a man. You have a lot of flexibility. Some of it is your own perseverance; sometimes you just stumble into it."

She continues: "There are people you meet along the way, and you get a break here or there. It might be an opportunity you were given that you may not realize is an opportunity until years later. But it's perseverance, sticking around, not making yourself obsolete, and how you approach your job that is unique.

"Most of us have learned from each other. If somebody has a better approach, asks a better question, or frames things a certain way, we'll adopt it. We may not do it consciously, but interaction with others is critical, in order to learn. Bouncing ideas off one another is critical to success. No one in the steel industry works and is operating independently of one another. It is one big family, and it is a family."

In her mind, being a family means that you look out for one another, and you also know one other. The name of the company may change but you still know each other. She was in the Armco mill in Butler, Pennsylvania, years ago. She had not visited that mill for a long time. When people heard she was visiting, they went out of their way to stop and say "Hi."

This comment about family is one I heard repeatedly throughout my interviews.

Ruth adds, "You need to always watch yourself because you will be remembered. No matter what you say, you will be remembered. This is not so much because you are a woman; it's the fact you are different. Different always sticks out."

Is there anything that women are more challenged with than men?

Ruth believes it takes longer to establish credibility, and if you are going into the steel mill, check *looking pretty* at the door, and make sure you have your safety equipment on.

Do you feel women approach their jobs differently than men?

She has noticed that some women have the idea they should be given a break because they are women, which is not going to endear them to anyone.

How did Armco support you in terms of personal or professional growth?

Ruth had to come up with different tactics to address this. She was not encouraged to attend the electric furnace division conventions or take continuing education courses. Realizing this, she would submit an abstract for a paper. When they accepted the abstract for the convention session, she told her boss that she needed to attend the conferences. Her boss always said "yes" to her requests. She would also say: "I will ask for all of these things, and your job is to tell me no."

While attending her first ISS Electric Division Convention, Ruth noticed there were no refractory sessions. So, Ruth offered to organize a session on refractories. The division chairman refused. However, before the conference concluded, the organizers approached her and told her if she could convince five people to submit papers for the next conference, they would agree to have a refractory session. She found five people to submit papers, and following that session the refractory committee became an ad-hoc committee for many years. Later on the refractory committee was granted official committee status.

Are there any generalities that people make about the steel industry?

Ruth feels the general population still relates the industry to an old TV show called *The Flintstones*, which featured cartoonish, prehistoric life.

Is there a quote or story that you have adopted or use as a personal mantra?

"Don't BS people. If you don't know something, say so and offer to investigate. Once a reputation is made, you can destroy it very easily."

* * *

Ruth ended our conversation by saying how much the steel industry has changed from when she first started in the industry and how it continues to evolve. The hot and cold mills operate very differently and attract different people with different approaches, and "it is a darn exciting place to work." She said that hot metal tends to attract people with strong opinions and even stronger personalities versus the cold end.

Ruth is charismatic in her own way. She prides herself on having created a life and career based on integrity, honesty, and hard work. Her curiosity far overrode any hesitancy she may have had initially about asking questions and she still is asking questions today.

This country was founded on offering opportunity and a new life to immigrants. This seventeen-year-old girl had a dream, and it was to graduate from high school and go to college here in the United States. She graduated with a master's degree, and the steel industry was fortunate to have this geology student who knew she could be successful in the material science area.

It was a privilege to interview Ruth for this book. I am proud to be able to highlight some of her achievements in the steel industry, but I also recognize a unique individual with a deep and profound respect for this industry.

Ruth has not only created a place for herself in the steel industry but within many industries.

Dr. Ruth *Is* in the house and her contributions will be recognized for a long time to come.

Thank you, Ruth.

About Refractory Consulting Services

Ruth Engel is the president of Refractory Consulting Services. Ruth provides services for refractory training, failure analysis, and process improvement for refractory life.

Although the majority of Engel's work is in steel, she consults with producers of aluminum, glass, silicon, copper, lime, dental implants, brick, and tile kiln companies and other refractory users. Engel's firm also works with legal and insurance companies.

To learn more, visit.refractoryexpert.com

CHAPTER TWO

Barbara R. Smith

Commercial Metals Company
Chairman, President and CEO

A Warrior's Heart

Within six months after Barbara joined Commercial Metals Company (CMC) as CFO, there was a hostile takeover attempt of the company by Carl Icahn. Barbara was new to the company and had not developed a working relationship with anyone.

While she knew what needed to be done during this crisis, she wasn't the decision maker; she wasn't the CEO. The stakes were high, probably the highest in her career, and during a critical presentation she looked out at the faces of three hundred of CMC's leaders and the families who were behind those faces and told herself, *we have to save this company.* That's when the warrior emerged.

During this crisis, her daughter had listened to her mom and dad discuss the situation. Their daughter was a sophomore in high school, and it had been her sixth move. Hearing the discussion, their daughter was concerned she would have to move yet again. One night at dinner, she asked her mom to explain what was going on at the company. As Barbara was attempting to explain what a hostile takeover was, her daughter interrupted her: "Stop. I get it, Mom. Are you scared?" No, honey, I'm not scared. There are just all of these people whose lives depend on this company carrying on."

"No offense," her daughter said, "but you are the biggest bitch I know. You can take him."

Barbara said she didn't know if she should wash her daughter's mouth out with soap or give her a hug! Afterward, she thought perhaps it was a compliment.

Barbara was born and raised in Lafayette, Indiana. Her mother was raised on a farm in Nebraska that is still in the family.

While one of Barbara's great-grandfathers was a coal miner in Pittsburgh, one of Barbara's grandfathers owned a fabricating shop. Although she never visited the shop, she finds it ironic she ended up in the metals industry. Her father even gifted her a set of andirons, which were hand-forged by her grandfather's business partner, as a wedding gift to her grandfather and grandmother.

Barbara is one of nine children—six girls, an older brother, and younger twin boys. As you might assume, a household of eleven people does not run itself! Everyone had a role to play in keeping the family machine working. There were always chores and never a distinction between a girl or boy task. She and her siblings were raised to believe: "You could do anything that you want to. It's just a question of putting your mind to it and being willing to work hard. I didn't grow up with a definition of what girls should do with their life."

She credits her midwestern background: "I just boil

it down to strong values and principles and a strong work ethic which has been so beneficial throughout my entire working career."

Her mother was an occupational therapist, an unusual degree for a woman at the time. But after the children were born, she chose to stay home. Barbara told me that both her mother and grandmother were very strong individuals. She was surprised when she discovered it was her grandmother who was the business mind behind the farm and it was her grandfather who loved the animals. Her mother and grandmother are among the nicest people she has known. Barbara has never heard either of them say an unkind word.

With nine children to feed and educate, her dad was involved in numerous business ventures that interested Barbara. She loved following her father around, particularly when he was working with tools. To this day, she can operate any power tool you give her!

She was always curious how products were made that are used in daily life. She had an opportunity to experience how things were built and made because her family did a lot of work and renovations around the house. Cars were purchased at auctions, torn apart, and rebuilt. The girls made their own clothes. She said they were a "do it yourself type of family."

Even with nine children in the family, it was assumed that each child would attend college. Barbara attended Purdue University and majored in business with a specialty in accounting. She worked throughout college mainly because she enjoyed working more than the classroom. During her junior and senior year, she worked full-time managing a boutique clothing shop, doing the buying, hiring, and training. She attended classes before the store opened and took night classes and summer courses.

Barbara was drawn to manufacturing and learning how products are produced. Her first job was with Alcoa in Tennessee, just outside of Knoxville. At this facility, Alcoa specialized in can sheet for beverages. Later, she realized that what she observed and learned at Alcoa translated over to the steel industry.

Her first job was as a systems analyst/computer programmer. At that time, data was being converted from manual files to computerized files through a coding language called COBOL. Barbara had taken one computer class at Purdue but didn't know anything about COBOL. Although Alcoa was willing to train her, Barbara—being resourceful—went to the library at the University of Tennessee, and along with several helpful IT people, taught herself how to code. These efforts earned her a great deal of respect within the department.

As everything was being automated, this training became a great foundation for Barbara. She spent three years working on accounting department systems. From there she became a cost accountant, which included tracking production costs and allocating costs to various products. She also interfaced with sales to help them understand how to price their products.

With thin margins in a cyclical business, identifying costs and being a low-cost producer were critical to the plant's success. As a result of her responsibilities, Barbara spent a great deal of time with the manufacturing group. Spending time on the manufacturing floor and doing the cost accounting work was invaluable to her.

"I was always more interested in what made the numbers rather than adding up the numbers and presenting them. I had this passion about what made the business work and how to translate what I was doing into helping management make business decisions. I was always more interested in the business side."

Were there many women working at the plant in 1981 when you started with Alcoa?

At the time there was a significant effort to increase the opportunities for women in all areas of the plant, particularly on the engineering side. The industry was very male dominated and still is, particularly in production.

Did you develop friendships with any of the women who joined the company?

One of the women she befriended is still her best friend. She stayed with Alcoa and recently retired.

Did the women stay and did you see other women being promoted?

Many of the women who joined Alcoa around 1981 in the Knoxville plant ended up leaving the organization once they started a family. However, there were women who joined the company and seemed able to balance both career and family.

Was there an expectation that the women would leave or that they would fail?

Barbara didn't think the women left due to male barriers but that it was a conscious decision to leave. She did feel that perhaps there could have been more accommodations made to encourage women with children to stay at the company. At the time, childcare options were limited. She had a child while she was working so felt it was a matter of personal choice.

Even with a desire to provide opportunities for women at Alcoa, she saw women assigned to positions that weren't a good fit, which led to attrition. Seeing this taught her that you must always fill the job with the most qualified person.

"We need to own our decisions. Individuals need to have a self-awareness of their deficiencies, blind spots, or lack of experience and reach out and build that support or fill in those gaps. If you don't, it isn't going to work."

In her early career, a few men were instrumental in her development and success. She didn't know what they saw in her, but they took an active interest in helping her succeed, whether it was taking extra time to explain or teach her something, give her advice, or help her prepare for a presentation or event.

What did you excel at that made people want to help you?

She says she is asked all the time what her path was, how she became successful and "what is the magic bullet."

"There is no magic bullet. I am not a quitter. Everyone's story is different. Everybody's path is different. Everybody had forks in the road they took. I go back to my work ethic. People will help you if they know you're going to jump in and do what it takes and you're willing to learn."

* * *

"I never saw barriers," she says, "only opportunities." She admits there were things that men did that weren't helpful. It was just the times. Never for one minute did she allow herself to become the victim of a negative mindset when the men didn't invite her to lunch or golf or include her in a business discussion.

She recognized that "being a woman, I could get things done in a different way that men couldn't. That was as powerful as all the indirect networking stuff, or choosing to focus on being a victim, or thinking there was a massive barrier. I would focus more on how to get things done and how to be effective based on me and my uniqueness. Everyone has barriers and obstacles. "

Barbara knew how to cook, use any power tool, ride a tractor, plow a field, and manage. Ten years into her career, she made baked goods around the holidays and brought them into work. One of the executives complimented her on what she had made, then took her aside and said: "Barbara, you can't let anyone know you made this. You're a woman in the workforce. You cannot let anybody know you cook."

She was taken aback by the executive's rationale that you can't cook and be

"I never saw barriers,
I only saw opportunities."

competent at work at the same time. She laughed and brought in more baked goods just to be cantankerous.

She left Tennessee to work at Alcoa's corporate headquarters in Pittsburgh, then went to a subsidiary in Nashville followed by an assignment where she commuted between Nashville and Cleveland for three years. She worked for Alcoa for twenty-four years and became one of the top fifty highest-ranking employees in the company. She realized when you get that high in an organization, there are fewer opportunities for advancement.

Barbara met her husband when she worked at Alcoa in Knoxville. They worked in different areas of the operation, and they were both successful. Her husband left Alcoa to work for the mayor of Knoxville. When they offered Barbara a position in Pittsburgh, she accepted, and Alcoa made an offer to her husband as well.

They were married for thirteen years before their daughter was born. At that time, both had well-established and successful careers. Their daughter was five years old when they offered Barbara the position in Nashville. By that time she was traveling around the world, and with a young daughter it was tough to juggle their schedules. She accepted the position in Nashville, with the understanding her husband would look for a new position since Alcoa did not have a position for him.

Their daughter wasn't quite ready to start kindergarten, so she and her dad spent their days together, sharing his passion for history and going on what her daughter called "field trips." At forty-nine, her husband put the job search on the back burner in exchange for days and experiences with his daughter. Pretty progressive and nontraditional.

Barbara looks back on this time as impactful both personally and professionally. With the help of her husband, she was able to accept promotions and job opportunities and not worry about balancing two high-profile careers and raising a daughter.

She says her husband is her number one fan. She acknowledges she couldn't do what she has done and continues to do without him. She feels he is an amazing man to have made the decision to step back from his career, but not his life. He has never looked back. According to Barbara, he is confident and comfortable with who he is and with his accomplishments. He is a great family man and loves spending time with his son (Barbara's stepson) and their daughter, who just graduated from law school. If she is honest with herself, she could be slightly jealous of the special bond that her daughter and husband share.

Barbara, her husband, and their daughter were living in Nashville while she commuted to Cleveland. They didn't want to move to Cleveland because her boss was working in New York City. She would eventually have to move to New York City and didn't want to move twice. She also didn't want to raise her daughter in the city. Her husband wasn't excited about New York either, so she began to look outside Alcoa.

She accepted a position as CFO with a fast-growing company called FARO Technologies. The company had $100M in annual sales and produces computer-aided, three-dimensional measurement devices that are used in manufacturing to eliminate rework and waste. Because the application was related to manufacturing, Barbara connected to the product.

It was a big risk for her at the time. She had some gaps in her experience because she had always been on the business side. She had no prior experience on the public-facing side including SEC reporting and investor relations. This opportunity would allow her to check a number of these boxes and become CFO of a publicly traded company.

Her transition into the steel industry from FARO Technologies came through a previous colleague at Alcoa, Mario Longhi. Mario had accepted a position at Gerdau Ameristeel in Tampa as President and CEO and asked her to join his team. While at Gerdau, the Brazilian parent company purchased 40 percent of the business that was public and took it private. Barbara recognized Gerdau would prefer their own management team and the company would not need her experience as a public company CFO.

Barbara almost accepted another position when an opportunity opened at CMC. She was familiar with their business, the markets, and the customers, and it felt like a good fit. CMC had some succession needs at the time and Barbara fit the requirements. Ten years later, she remains excited about the potential of the company, management team, employees, and their direction forward.

How did the company respond to the COVID-19 crisis?

It turns out she contracted COVID-19 herself. As a CEO it was hard for her to take the time to rest and recover, the downside of being the boss. She is very complimentary of how the leadership and management teams at CMC handled this crisis.

"Their instincts were so good. They immediately implemented procedures to keep employees safe. They were

constantly evaluating the information and putting protocols in place. We organized a task force at corporate
that oversaw broad company-wide issues. It was great
to see how the team quickly mobilized in response to a
crisis. They were decisive and knew instinctively what
needed to be done."

Barbara centered her focus around keeping her employees safe, keeping the business running, and protecting
the business for the short and long term. She wanted
to make sure that employees' jobs and income were
protected. Employees were told they would be paid
and to not worry if they contracted COVID-19. Management was very concerned about new demands on
their employees such as remote school, childcare issues,
extended caregiver issues, and employees' feelings
concerning vaccination. She is pleased with how the
management team responded. They tried to be as
consistent as they could across the business.

What is your definition of success?

"It's enjoying what you do without feeling like you are
trying to compete with someone else. So many people
are just putting in time. Every job has pleasant and
unpleasant tasks. I get more fulfillment and joy out of
watching other people be successful and seeing how I
influenced or helped shape them."

Barbara experienced how competitive law school was
through her daughter and her daughter's friends who
had just graduated. She advised them that after they
started to work, they were going to begin to compare themselves and their progress to one another.

She cautioned them that not everyone's career would move at the same pace and that each of them would be confronted with forks in the road and different choices. She suggested they had two alternatives; be happy and supportive of their friends' successes or be jealous. She said if you choose to be happy for other people's successes, then that is success. If you choose to constantly compare yourself to others or are always looking toward the next thing, you are not appreciating the moment, or your achievements.

"Everyone can find success. It's different for everyone. It's a combination of your whole life. You fall down, you pick yourself up. To me, success is if you can be happy doing whatever it is you're doing, and not looking at someone else and want what they have."

What is your definition of failure?

"It's becoming a victim. There are plenty of things that we fail at in life, but the minute you get consumed with regrets, or use the excuse that this happened to me because somebody did something to me, it's a victim mindset and very destructive. Failure is a barrier to the opposite, which is success."

What is your definition of happiness?

"I am a simple person. I can be happy doing anything." She remembers reading that "happiness is a conscious choice."

Barbara and her husband moved their daughter six times in fifteen years, and her daughter felt she didn't have a place to call home. The family had owned beach property for twenty years and that was home to her daughter because it was always there, it was always the same. It came to a point when the family wasn't using the beach house and discussed selling the property. Her daughter became emotional and Barbara explained to her that it is not the physical place that is special, but the memories, who you are with, and what you are doing that make it special and creates traditions.

Barbara says there are lots of days that she can come up with all kinds of reasons not to be happy. "You need to make a conscious choice to not go that direction and not let the days, weeks, months, and years of burdens take you to a different place. I just think family, little things like tradition, all those things make me happy."

What is the difference between a manager and a leader?

"When I think of the word *manager*, I think of assigning tasks, telling people what to do, and checking things off a list. A leader is someone who defines and sets goals and direction for the organization. They define the ground rules and help the group understand their role in achieving success. While providing resources, coaching, and feedback to accomplish the goal, you get out of the way. Once you achieve the goal, a leader will celebrate, reward the team, and provide feedback."

On CMC's website, I noticed a series of 350 online training programs including leader and management development programs. Barbara, what do we need to do as an industry to create more leaders?

She is fascinated with the steel industry. During the late 1990s, the industry was in distress and many of the steel businesses were struggling. It was the last place anyone who was talented would want to work. Then you layer in the stigma around the industry on top of that.

Barbara says: "We need to redefine what it means to have a career in this industry. It also starts with having success. The industry has consolidated and modernized. You can have as rewarding and success-ful career in this industry as you can in high-tech. It's incumbent on us, and we are not there yet, to redefine what a career in this industry looks like. Yes, we wear blue jeans and some of us work on the factory floor, but what is wrong with that? It's showing the level of technology that is applied and we get people involved in implementing that technology and those processes early in their careers. Individuals can have a very rewarding career if you can get past the old industry stigma."

Barbara added that as far as attracting diverse new leaders, you need some success stories. She hopes she is viewed as an example that young women can look to; and realize, if she can do it, I can do it. It is not a prize that is out of reach.

In order to facilitate this redefinition of the industry and CMC, the company changed their website and other public documents consistent with their modern and technologically advanced operations. They focused on recycling, sustainability, and presenting a com-pelling message to the public in an effort to interest young people to consider working at CMC and joining the steel industry. "We have to change the message, tell the story a different way. The companies in this industry are fabulous companies using unbelievably advanced technology."

When she became somewhat frustrated with how to redefine what it means to be in this industry, and be a target of unwanted and biased opinions from the public, one of her board members suggested: "Tell the story the way your story needs to be told, not the way somebody is going to spin the story and tell it."

This advice resonated with Barbara. She realized that CMC has a great story to tell and shared one of their success stories with me. Unlike a lot of techie-type businesses that can physically disappear in twenty-four to forty-eight hours, building a steel mill is an investment. According to Barbara, a mill is a "fifty-year decision." CMC wanted to build a new mill to support growth in the south-central United States. After researching sites, the team chose to build the $350M mill in Durant, Oklahoma—a town in the middle of the Choctaw nation. When Barbara first visited the area, she was overwhelmed with how economically depressed it was. This town haunted Barbara. When she left and came back she said, "We are going to do something good for this community."

As construction began, you started to see the impact that hundreds of site workers had on the local economy. Workers were eating and living in town, shopping at Walmart, spending their money. As Barbara says, "The town started to come alive."

She also described how CMC partnered with the Choctaw nation to build this plant. Their chief, Gary Batton, had a vision of providing higher-paying jobs that were different from the entertainment jobs at the local casino.

Of course, other businesses have located in and around Durant, as a result of CMC's investment and the vision of local officials. She said the town has been completely transformed. CMC employees have rolled up their sleeves and become involved in the community. They support local events and are spending their money and investing in the local economy.

"People take such pride in working for the company. In these communities, our name is appreciated, because when we show up, we show up with everything." CMC

Barbara Smith, mill dedication in Durant, Oklahoma 2018.
(Photo courtesy of AIST archives)

didn't just provide jobs at their factory to the people in Durant, Oklahoma, and the surrounding area, they provided hope and life to a town and created pride.

How many of your executive leadership team are women?

"We have six people on the team, half of whom are women. In management, 25 percent of the leadership positions are held by women. More than 50 percent of the overall employee population is comprised of women and ethnically diverse individuals." She says they still have a lot of opportunities on the production side where men outnumber women. She is pleased with the progress being made to create diversity within the company and very proud of how CMC is addressing this.

Do you notice any differences between men and women in the executive level versus the management level?

"The combination of men and women, recognizing the differences and the strength of those differences and how they can be complementary, is powerful if people can put it to work. Women seem to approach situations differently than men. Women generally have great attention to detail, are very organized and goal-oriented. If a woman commits to something, that commitment is not easily broken."

What are your thoughts and experiences with mentoring?

Barbara has been involved in formalized and informal mentoring, both of which have their merits. She has been in successful formalized mentoring programs and some mentoring situations that were awkward and less effective. What she found is not effective is a forced relationship where there is no passion on one side or both sides for the process and the results.

During her first ten years with Alcoa there were one or two individuals who supported and mentored her. Sometimes, it was a boss who took a special interest in her or someone who fought for her when new job openings or opportunities became available. In some cases, they helped promote her from behind the scenes, which she didn't discover until years later.

CMC does a lot of mentoring both informally and formally, particularly with new employees. It might be something subtle like taking a new employee out to lunch to find out how they are doing or if they are struggling. Someone might be asked to watch over someone and provide positive and constructive feedback on their performance.

On a more formal basis, CMC starts with a leadership assessment that identifies an individual's strengths and weaknesses. Then they find a program to match the needs of the employee. For example, is there a need for more constructive feedback, more compassion and empathy, or more authenticity and vulnerability? Maybe there is a need for more communication and inspirational leadership. They utilize a myriad of ways to help employees expand their strengths and become successful.

What are three pivotal experiences that have influenced you?
I suggested the story behind the facility in Durant,

Oklahoma, and working with Chief Gary Batton. She agreed.

She also mentioned the hostile takeover attempt by Carl Icahn. She knew there had been some business decisions made that put the company in a rocky financial position prior to her coming to CMC, but she didn't know the full story until she joined the company.

Rather than go away, the situation was exacerbated by unfavorable market conditions that left the company financially vulnerable, making it difficult to meet the financial commitments.

She had just moved into her home and was unpacking boxes when everything came to a head and became a full-blown crisis. The only way to fulfill the financial obligations was to lever up the company. There she was, the CFO depending on the CEO. Barbara said that you either have significant influence in a situation or you are trying to keep the CEO from doing something drastic. Barbara was the keeper of the numbers; everything had to be correct. But she knew she was an influencer, not the key decision-maker.

The organization became paralyzed and was uncertain how to move forward.

Barbara knew she had to make everyone understand the numbers. She created charts that identified the cash flow and identified steps needed to get out of the crisis. They marshaled the troops and laid out a very detailed plan. The plan was very specific. If not executed perfectly, Carl Icahn would control the company.

Barbara remembers a pivotal meeting that included three hundred members from the leadership teams at CMC. She had her time slot to present the numbers. Remember, she had only been at the company a little more than a few months. She created what would later be known as "the scary chart." She explained the financial situation in a very calm and simplistic way.

She remembers staring at the faces in the audience and thinking, *We can't lose this fight.* She knew Carl Icahn would disassemble the company, and an untold number of people would lose their jobs and their ability to support their families. The faces that were looking at her were such a motivation for her, and she had no idea the impact she would have on them by simply presenting the truth. After her presentation, she said, "They went, and they executed. We gave the team the next list to execute, and the next list, and the teams did everything they were supposed to do." CMC defeated the hostile takeover effort from Carl Icahn.

What Barbara finds heartening about this story is that no one knew her. The management and leadership teams could have rejected her efforts because she was an outsider. Instead, they believed what she'd said, without question, and they won! She says she knew what to do, she had their best interests at heart, and it was never about her. To this day, ten years later, people still bring up that meeting. They still mention the "scary chart," and they thank her for what she did. She doesn't remember a word she said while she explained the numbers at that meeting, but she will always remember their faces and telling them the truth.

This crisis brought the company together in ways that would have taken years to accomplish.

What did you learn about yourself through this crisis and through your career?

She says it reinforced her level of determination, resilience, and perseverance. She also learned to be vulnerable. Barbara admits she is an introvert, a trait that many CEOs share. In kindergarten, her teacher told her mother that she wouldn't amount to anything because she was so shy in school. To become more vulnerable and open was a stretch for her, particularly because—like many of us—she was raised in a midwestern household where she was told not to discuss private family business outside the family.

When she started in 1981, women were stereotyped as very emotional. For the first half of her life, the career push was to beat the emotive side out of you. You had to be stoic and under control. You couldn't pound the table or get angry. She learned she had to do it a different way.

She explained that when you begin to be promoted, you are trying to win the hearts and minds of the people who are making those decisions. They want to know the person behind the face. This was made more challenging because of the stoic and "buttoned-up" conditioning she had when she first started with Alcoa, and I might add, we had when we first started in the steel industry. At Gerdau she was called the "Ice Queen," which alluded to her ability to be cool under fire, but she was actually taken aback by that title. You can understand why vulnerability has been a challenge for her.

Did you ever feel you were underpaid during your career?
She felt she was fortunate to work with great companies and did not experience pay inequity.

She is very pleased with her VP-HR at CMC. She and Barbara have been diligent to make sure there are no inequities within the company. They have conducted gender, diversity, and pay equity studies and she admits the results have been fascinating because of the science behind these exercises. In CMC's studies, the results were very rewarding in a positive way. Any inequities found were due to time in the role or other explainable reasons.

Do you see any barriers to attracting women into the steel industry?
She sees the stigma around heavy manufacturing and the environment as a factor. She says CMC has no trouble attracting talent to their corporate headquarters in Dallas, Texas, and is proud that they have the reputation as a great employer due to their culture, diversity, and people. The company is a big recycler and has promoted the sustainable nature of the business. She admits it is more challenging in operations because of shift work and the mill environment, which does create some barriers for women. She doesn't make any excuses. She says we have to do better and overcome these barriers. She says they have more work to do in this area.

What are some of CMC's biggest challenges going forward?

She feels it is important that strategically the company identifies the right kind of growth. If it is an acquisition, you need the right fit.

Since the industry has consolidated, the opportunities for growth are not as plentiful as they were ten years ago. She has seen companies chase growth for the sake of growth even though it doesn't fit strategically.

Another issue that is concerning to the entire industry, not only CMC, is the topic of succession. The steel industry has an aging workforce. Preparing the next group of leaders and management has become an urgent issue.

The industry has been growing and so has CMC. This has created opportunities to move people into new jobs that require new skills. You need a different approach to not only promote the industry, but to promote the company. It is a much more dynamic environment now than when she started with Alcoa.

The last area she sees as a challenge is what she calls the "macro government environment." Government policies are very impactful on the steel industry. She said we have had two administrations with different approaches to trade and the industry. She said the industry simply wants a level playing field with the rest of the world. There is a lot of rhetoric around the government environment, which seems more committed to pulling groups apart rather than bringing them together.

43

As a leader of a public company, Barbara is concerned about all her employees. She feels there is a lot of pressure to speak out on public issues with the right balance, the right message, the right dance. She does not want to divide her workforce. She shared an impactful statement she once heard: "Everyone is unique, precious, and unrepeatable."

If everyone would believe this, she feels we would get along better and be more effective at solving problems. Focusing on the positive instead of the negative, and on what we have in common versus what we don't have in common, is most important.

＊ ＊ ＊

We concluded our interview with acknowledging her award from AIST as Steelmaker of the Year in 2019.

*Barbara accepting Steelmaker of the Year Award 2019
from 2018-2019 AIST President James Dudak*

This is a coveted award in the industry and the plaque read, "For her leadership and strategic evolution of CMC through fostering a corporate culture of safety, community and customer service, investment in a second continuous process mini-mill in Oklahoma, introducing spooled rebar into the North American market and maintaining high customer satisfaction and profitability in the challenging long products market. Smith has positioned CMC as an industry leader."

This award is particularly meaningful to her because participants are nominated and selected by peers. CMC employees nominated her and organized the entire submission, without her knowledge. She says the employees were proud to see her and CMC recognized at this level.

She is also very proud of being selected as an "Old Master" of Purdue University. This honor comes with a rigorous nomination process. Students research outstanding alumni and, if selected, are invited to the main campus along with other "Old Masters" selected that year for a weekend of activities. She was thrilled to be included in this special group of amazingly accomplished and successful group of individuals.

Other awards that she and CMC have received recently: ranked one of the Top 100 Places to Work by the *Dallas Morning News* (2020 and 2021); *Dallas Morning News'* Best Direction Award for sound strategy and clear communication to all team members (2021); recognized by Women's Forum of New York as a 2021 Corporate Champion for having achieved 35 percent or more female board representation; S&P Global Platts CEO of the Year Award (2020); recognized by Women on Boards for having at least 20 percent women on the Board of Directors (2020); awarded Good

Employer Award XIII National Program of Corporate Social Responsibility (2019); received the Steel Manufacturers Association's Achievement in Innovation Award (2019)

What is your vision or passion for the industry?

"We have a really unique opportunity to redefine the industry." She recently participated on a global task force that presented recommendations on employment and education from companies around the world. The goal was to identify three or four key areas that the G20 countries should attack as it relates to employment and education. One of the topics focused on the subject of violence against women in the workplace, something we addressed in the United States years ago.

She then quoted the statistic that 70 percent of the steel produced in the United States is produced from recycled scrap versus the rest of the world where 70 percent of steel is produced from iron ore. The United States has the lowest greenhouse gas emissions in the world, and we have the lowest energy consumption in the world. We invest millions of dollars annually to innovate and improve the impact that the industry has on the environment because it makes good business sense. She compares the United States to China where they continue to pollute the air, the water, and their food stream with little regard for human life.

She feels passionate about the need for a vibrant manufacturing industry in this country, particularly in steel. We need to educate and tell the story about the importance of manufacturing in this country and that people should be as familiar with manufacturing as they are with Facebook and Google.

* * *

Yes, Barbara has a warrior's heart. CMC and this industry are fortunate to have her at the helm and ready to fight these battles.

Thank you, Barbara.

About CMC

Founded in 1915, CMC is a global leader in sustainable recycling, manufacturing, and fabrication of steel and metal products, and is a leading provider of construction reinforcement solutions. CMC's products go mostly unseen but help to build and support virtually every element of modern life—from highways, bridges, and airports to skyscrapers, sports stadiums, and hospitals.

Headquartered in Dallas, Texas, CMC's unique vertical integration business model revolutionized how the steel industry operates today. Originally founded as a metal recycling business, the company has continued to incorporate sustainable business practices as they have grown. CMC manufactures steel using 100 percent recycled scrap metal and electric arc furnace (EAF) technology, which is far more efficient and environmentally friendly than traditional blast furnace technology.

As a forward thinker and an innovator in the materials sector, CMC continues to discover new ways to further advance production processes and is leading the development of sustainable construction products.

To learn more, visit cmc.com.

Anna Mareschi Danieli

Danieli Group
Vice Chairwoman Steelmaking Division

A Grandfather's Vision and a Matriarch's Legacy Live On

T he history of the Danieli Group is a story unto itself. I had the opportunity to interview Mrs. Anna Mareschi Danieli. She is forty years young and is the vice chairwoman of the steelmaking division at Danieli in Buttrio, Italy.

What I found fascinating was the impact her mother had on Anna and on the company. In 1985, Anna's mother, Cecilia Danieli, was elected chairwoman of the board of Danieli.

Her mother died of cancer in 1999, at the age of fifty-five, two days before Anna and her twin brother's high school graduation. Anna and her twin brother were only eighteen. Her mother had a tremendous influence on Anna's personal and professional life, and to this day Anna still finds strength, direction, and wisdom from her influence. While Mr. Gianpietro Benedetti, her mother's longtime business partner, friend, and shareholder in the company, and Anna's twin brother Giacomo create the vision and path for the future of the company, it is Anna who inherited her mom's core role in administration and finance.

Were you expected to join Danieli and become active in the company?

Anna explained that her mother had a very clear picture of what her future would look like. Anna remembers when she was thirteen or fourteen years old, her mother told her she would attend Bocconi University in Milan, and major in business administration and finance. Her brother was going to go to the best engineering university in Milan, like his grandfather before him. Anna never questioned what her mother envisioned for her, and didn't even think to consider any alternatives. She is convinced that the mere fact of having a great opportunity requires pursuing it.

"Failing is the best way to success."

Anna saw firsthand the sacrifices her mother made as chairwoman of Danieli and appreciates the personal and professional cost of those sacrifices. Anna's mother told her, "If you have an opportunity, a good opportunity, a big opportunity, you need to take it. It is your moral obligation to take it, with the necessity to be part of something important." Since Anna became a mom of three, she understands the sacrifices you make when you choose those "big opportunities," but she is not certain anymore if it is always the right direction to go. Anna is still balancing these often conflicting responsibilities out in her own mind but strives to be the best possible mother to her children.

If your mother gave you a choice of what career you would like to pursue, what would you have chosen?

Anna said she probably would have chosen to be a doctor. However, being a physician was not an option for her. Her mother's commitment to continuing the family legacy and maybe to some extent her own legacy as a successful businesswoman far outweighed Anna's voice. Anna accepted her decision with enthusiasm.

Anna aims to raise and educate her daughter to be a strong and independent woman like her mother, as she did with her.

What were some of the sacrifices your mother made as a working mom and chairman of the company?

Her mother frequently traveled internationally. Since travel was not as convenient then as it is today, her mother could be gone for two or three months at a time, particularly when she traveled to China.

Although her mother sincerely wanted to attend Anna's birthdays, she was rarely present. She had many business commitments and told her daughter, "Customer is King." Every time she missed an important occasion, her mother promised Anna that she would be there for her eighteenth birthday. Unfortunately, fate got in the way. Her mother was not able to celebrate her eighteenth birthday with her and died a few months later at the age of fifty-five.

As a mom herself, Anna knows from experience when children need their mother. It is heartbreaking when a mother can't be with her children. I asked Anna how she was balancing her roles as a business executive and mother since she is expected to travel around the world. When she goes to India, she tries to complete the trip in forty-eight hours. She doesn't get a lot of rest, but the jam-packed schedule allows her to accomplish what she needs to and minimizes the time she is away from her children.

Due to the pressures of her career, she focuses on quality time versus quantity time with her children and that is the example she is choosing to set for her children. Anna remembers that because her mother traveled so frequently, she never wanted to go out to dinner when she returned home from her business trips. Anna recalls begging her mom to take her out for dinner, but she never would, so Anna makes a point of taking her children out to dinner.

When Anna would complain to her mother because she wanted more of her attention, she would tell Anna, "Remember that I don't have only three kids; I have five thousand." Anna witnessed her mother's compassion for her employees. If an employee was troubled, hurting, or alone, her mother felt committed to helping that person. She would take time to sit and listen to their problems and concerns. It is this same care and concern for employees that Anna tries to emulate on a daily basis.

When Anna would ask her mom to sit with her, she would say, "Remember that you are already lucky enough to be my daughter, so leave something for others." In other words, her mom was telling her children that because of their privileged place in the world and because they were safe and loved, they needed to share their mother. The idea that others were not so fortunate is a difficult concept for a little girl to comprehend. As an adult, Anna understands this was a powerful lesson she learned from her mother and is deeply committed to following her profound teaching.

After graduating with her degree in business administration, Anna went into investment banking. Her mother had been a chief financial officer prior to her becoming chairwoman of Danieli. Anna wanted to follow in her footsteps.

* * *

At that time, as a prerequisite to working at The Investment Bank in Italy, you had to have completed an internship in the financial or banking field and be proficient in two languages. To satisfy that requirement, Anna elected to go to South Carolina for one year and did her internship in the steel industry with CMC. After her internship, she accepted a position in Paris for two years, then returned to Italy and worked for two years in Unicredit SpA, an Italian financial bank. She finally went back to Buttrio and began working for Danieli. During her first five years at Danieli, she frequently traveled to India because "no one else wanted to go." Using her financial background, she became responsible for the financing and contracting department and for monitoring cash flow for the group.

Anna is just finishing a four-year term as the first woman president of Confindustria Udine, the main association representing manufacturing and service companies in Italy. This is a formidable private Italian association whose activities are aimed at continuing to guarantee the central importance of companies and businesses that drive Italy's economic, social, and civil development. She was pleased to be the first woman to hold this position in the organization in her region, and to see so many women representing different economic sectors throughout Italy. "We have to push for these things; otherwise, we will never leave a better world to our daughters." She says she is "fighting a lot in this field" because it is still a man's world.

Anna went on to talk about the other battles she is fighting. She says you can't pass through the transition to equality if "you don't recognize the big role a mother plays in society. It is not only about care." She stated that many of the underlying cultural and traditional responsibilities around family still fall on the woman in the family to manage; for example, childcare, doctor's appointments, caring for aged parents or extended family members, and so on. But, according to Anna, this issue has a financial impact on businesses and needs a bigger political platform for discussion and action.

What is your maternity leave for women in Italy?
In Italy a woman has five months' paid maternity leave, which Anna supports. She says she wouldn't have an issue if that time was extended and included paternity leave for men.

Are you required to hire women in your company, and how many women work in management at Danieli?
Anna says that government legislation in this area only applies to boardrooms and the executive levels. At Danieli, approximately ten percent of their middle management and executive management are female. "As long as a law is needed to guarantee a human right, it will mean that we are still a long way from equality."

Anna feels if a company needs to choose between hiring a woman or a man who have the exact same qualifications and competencies, they prefer to hire the man. She added that the man is in a position to give more time to the job because he doesn't have the responsibility and cultural pressures of taking care of children, parents, and extended family members. Many women are forced to use their paid and unpaid leave caring for others. Men are more available to travel, can work longer hours because they don't have the added responsibilities of taking care of the children, families, etc. According to Anna, the answer to equalizing this imbalance could be a fiscal approach. For example, she feels a company shouldn't have to pay taxes on women with children, employees on maternity leave, or those who are on disability.

What are some of your biggest challenges?

Obviously, balancing her professional and personal life is and will continue to be a challenge for Anna. She puts one of the challenges in a much bigger socio-economic arena with a focus on Italian culture. Within this culture is a pervasive bias to teach girls that they need to be perfect, go to college, excel academically, and not move too far from their families and the communities where they were raised. In her opinion, girls should be raised to be strong, and to learn to be risk-takers.

"Failing is the best way to success." She feels that girls need to learn this when they are young because otherwise it becomes problematic as an adult. She admits that overcoming feelings of guilt is a personal challenge for her. If she works too much she feels guilty not being at home with her children. If she takes time for her children she feels guilty being away from work. "It's an endless vicious circle for a mom." As a result, Anna's sense of responsibility and fear of failure makes her feel that she needs to work harder than anyone else, which is a daily challenge.

What is your definition of failure?

She says her grandfather failed in business three times before founding Danieli. He credited the impact from WWI and WWII for two of those failures. However, her grandfather had a vision of what he wanted to create and realized that "failure was a part of getting there." Her grandfather and all successful entrepreneurs learn from failures and what failure teaches you.

What is your definition of success?
"Success is a happy and well-educated child who greets you when you come home from work in the evening." She says when you are successful you don't take the time to savor the success, to be happy and grateful for the success. Instead, you are already on to the next goal, the next project, the next moment. She doesn't think that thought process will ever stop for her.

What is your definition of happiness?
Happiness is a state of mind. "If you want to be happy, you find the way to be happy as long as you have good health." Anna feels you need to be satisfied with what you have and not be too materialistic.

What are you most proud of?
She is most proud of her three children, the youngest being one year old. She had been up since 3:30 a.m. the day we talked, and she said coffee was helping her get through the day.

When she was younger, she never thought she would have children and she was okay with that. Her mother had told her that if you can't afford them, don't have children. Her mom struggled after Anna's parents divorced.

What have you learned about yourself?

The number one thing she has learned about herself is that even if your are heartbroken, you won't die. "Everything else you can handle." She mentioned how drastically her life changed when she was eighteen after her mother died. Her mother "was the most important person" in her life. And in a few months she wasn't there anymore. Her parents had divorced when she was two years old so it was just her and her two brothers. She says, "Even if your life is completely destroyed, the world still goes on. In the beginning this makes you so angry but after a while you get used to it." This is a difficult life lesson when you are eighteen.

The second thing she has learned is about managing life and "how much more difficult it is to think about managing your life than to actually manage your life." Oftentimes, it is easier to jump in and do things versus thinking about how difficult something could be.

What do you bring to the company and your job that is unique?

The company legacy is a huge part of that uniqueness. Anna says she surrounds herself with people who are smarter than she is. "You don't lose your authority when you do this. We don't have to be scared of people's minds." She sees strength and opportunity for the company when you utilize and respect employees' inherent talents. She wants other people in the company to adopt this same mindset.

What has been your impact on the company?

She feels the difference she can make is to "use the power to be a woman." When I asked her to explain, she said originally she "was not taken seriously in the beginning. You have to work hard to be taken seriously." Once everyone knows you are serious then it becomes easier to be accepted.

What do you think women bring to the job that is different?

Anna doesn't like to answer this question. She feels it categorizes men and women and differentiates one from the other—what she explains as giving fuel to the diversity issue. She hates when people ask her about "the pink side of steel." Anna says that every employee should be able to bring their best game to the table regardless of whether they are female or male.

What is your definition of a manager versus a leader, and what is Danieli doing to continue as an industry leader?

The difference between a manager and a leader is authority. Her mother used to say, "It is better to be a good shareholder than a bad manager." In other words, if you can't lead, get out of the way of your ego, and let someone lead who can.

Anna says that Danieli's philosophy comes from a long-term commitment to investing in research and technology, and you need state-of-the-art technology to be successful. Over the last ten years they have invested more than $1B Euros in technology.

Something else Anna learned from her mother is that everyone in the company is family, and management should understand that employees need a life outside of work.

What interests you about this book?

Without categorizing men and women in the industry, she feels it is good to let people outside the industry know there are successful women in the industry. These women are every bit as capable and effective as the men. Secondly, it is important to present and discuss different job opportunities and pathways that are available to women and young men in the industry.

What are some pivotal experiences you have had?

Obviously, losing her mother at eighteen was a monumental experience, but so was the influence that her mother had on her as a mother and as the head of Danieli.

Anna discovered in her experiences, "You don't need to be a genius to do things. You just need to have courage."

Anna remembers in 2008 when she first joined Danieli as a financial specialist and was visiting a challenging customer in New Delhi. He was keeping the Danieli team working late hours, weekends, and holidays. He would not speak to Anna directly because she was a woman and addressed her colleague instead. It took three weeks of her showing this customer that she was dedicated and knowledgeable before he began to speak to her directly and shake her hand. Anna, who was twenty-seven at the time, realized through this experience her customer's culture was the reason he reacted to her in that way.

"What is difficult is to have faith and continue to try," she says. "If you are going to change someone's attitude, you do so through your behavior and letting the customer see that you are there to help solve a problem or create an opportunity and work together." Through her actions, she convinced the customer that he should be doing business with Danieli. It was a win for her and a pivotal experience at twenty-seven years old.

How do you see you and your brother moving the company forward?

Anna knows her brother has many skills including his technical skills as an engineer, and she has the financial skills. She feels this is a good balance for now, but cannot say today what will be best for the company tomorrow.

What are some generalities that people still make about the business?

A lot of people still think the steel industry represents old technology. "We are in the future, more so than a lot of other sectors." She is astounded that people still view the industry in this way. She explained that Danieli recently commissioned a new wire rod mill that requires no people to be on the floor of the mill.

What is the greatest contribution you have made so far within the company?

"My competencies and myself in general. I cannot give anything more. This is all I have."

How did Danieli handle COVID-19?

At the time of our interview, all of Danieli's facilities were operational and following strict protocols. She said not everyone in her region had been vaccinated due to lack of availability of the vaccine. She made one interesting speculation about the steel industry and COVID-19. Anna says that since the industry maintains strict safety practices to begin with, they, as a whole, already had a lot of safety protocols in place. But overall, the industry has managed COVID-19 and safety protocols better than a lot of other sectors.

How can we attract more women into the industry, and what are some of the reasons there are not more women in business and industry?

Anna said the demographics for Italy are quite concerning. Italy has not had any population growth over the last three decades. In the next fifteen years there will be two aged citizens for every young person, which is not sustainable. She feels that all industries need to be more motivated to hire women.

From a political perspective, the government needs to recognize that women have two jobs, one job as an employee and the second job as a mother and caretaker of the family. More services need to be provided to the families to incentivize women to work while raising a family.

I asked Anna if she sees a trend toward men staying home to raise and take care of the children while their wives work. "Absolutely not." She says that is not a trend in Italy. With a five-month maternity leave in Italy, Anna believes that companies should not have to pay federal and state taxes while women are on maternity leave or disability leave. She calls it the "de-fiscalization" of mothers in the workplace. I think Anna has created a new term.

Anna described her personal situation. While she loves her children, she chose to work and needs a babysitter to care for them. Because she can't afford not to be at the company, she has a primary babysitter and a secondary babysitter available at all times. In the event the primary babysitter becomes ill or can't be there she has "the backup plan." Obviously, this is expensive. She says that is why so few women are in high positions in Italy because of the economics of this situation. She says, "If you are going to be chairman of something, you need to give 110 percent of your time to that." She feels women can't make that commitment if they are constantly being pulled away from work to handle childcare and other family obligations and responsibilities.

This situation presents several other issues as well. When children spend so much time with a babysitter, they sometimes prefer to be with their caregiver rather than their parents. The second issue is the continual influence of the sitter on the children. Phrases, manners of speech, ideas, concepts—all of these affect the children. Then there is the guilt and jealousy that arises when your children prefer spending time with the sitter versus time with their mother. Anna's mother dealt with this situation, and Anna is confronted with it now.

Do you have any funny stories?

After the birth of her twins it was very challenging for Anna. Not only is one baby a big adjustment but two is an even bigger adjustment, especially if they are on different schedules. She had a dog at the time who became very agitated and unsettled after the babies came home from the hospital. Anna took the dog to the vet, who prescribed anti-anxiety medication to calm the dog and help the dog deal with the stress.

Here is Anna, with twin babies, sleep-deprived, anxious, and stressed herself, and she ends up needing to give the dog anxiety medication.

What would people like to know about you?

She says "nothing interesting" in her opinion." She says she is a totally normal person.

Anna wanted to convey to the readers of this book that "we really don't have to be perfect because nobody is." The most important thing we can do in our life is to have well-educated and happy children."

❋ ❋ ❋

Anna is far from a totally normal person and far from, in her words, "nothing interesting." She is resourceful and successful professionally and personally. She and her brother have inherited the legacy of an internationally recognized family business built by her grandfather and her mother, whose influence remains and guides her to this day.

Thank you, Anna, for this time together, especially since you had been up since 3:30 a.m.

About Danieli Group

Danieli Group is an Italian supplier of equipment and physical plants to the metal industry. The company is based in Buttrio, in the very north-east of Italy (Friuli-Venezia-Giulia region). It is one of the world leaders in the production of steel plants, in particular in the long products segment, where it owns more than a 90% market share.

Danieli was founded in 1914 when the brothers Mario and Timo Danieli, originally from Valsugana, acquired the Angelini Steelworks in Brescia. They were among the first Italian companies to use electric arc furnaces to produce steel. After WWI the two brothers separated. In 1929 Mario moved to Buttrio to produce steel processing equipment and auxiliary machines for rolling plants. After WWII, the company, led by Mario's son, Luigi, was renamed Danieli & Company and concentrated on the production of machines for the steel industry.

In 1984 the company was listed on the Milan Stock Exchange.

In the mid-1980s the steel sector encountered difficulties again and the company decided to adopt a different strategy to remain competitive: Cecilia Danieli and Gianpietro Benedetti pushed for a strong restructuring, in line with a strategy of internationalization and expansion of products.

In June 1999 Cecilia Danieli died in Aviano. The New York Times referred to her as "the Steel Lady."

Today the company has more than twenty-five divisions worldwide (design, manufacturing, and service centers), seven of which are production centers. Their facilities are located in Italy, Russia, Austria, Brazil, Netherlands, Sweden, United States, Vietnam, Germany, India, China, and Thailand.

Source: Wikipedia

To learn more, visit danieli.com or danieli-usa.com

CHAPTER FOUR

Carol R. Jackson

*HarbisonWalker International, Inc
Chairman of the Board, President and Chief
Executive Officer*

"I am going to be a CEO by the age of 40."

I n her senior high school yearbook, Carol wrote, "I am going to be a CEO of a multi-national company by the age of forty." She missed that goal by only a few years.

She credits her home, family life, and Junior Achievement for giving her the understanding and confidence to create that goal for herself. Junior Achievement is a nonprofit global program educating students from kindergarten to twelfth grade about entrepreneurship, financial literacy, and work/career readiness.

Carol's dad was head of Human Resources for Rockwell International and her mother worked in the insurance industry. Carol is proud of where she came from. Her family lived on a farm. It wasn't a working farm, more of a hobby farm. On Saturday mornings, she and her sister would go to church for handbell choir practice, come home, change their clothes, and work all afternoon on the farm. They might be asked to drive a tractor, mow grass, tend cattle—anything that their dad needed them to do. It was hard work, but "at the end of the day, you look back and feel good about what you've done."

She had a small, close family, and never had babysitters. If her parents went somewhere, it was her grandparents who babysat. She had two sets of grandparents—the city grandparents and the country grandparents. She differentiated them by the TV shows they were allowed to watch when they were with them. The country grandparents watched *Hee Haw*, a country-western music variety show, and the city grandparents watched *The Lawrence Welk Show*, a televised musical show hosted by a well-known big band leader. She said she had the best of both worlds and learned to appreciate and respect diversity due to the differences she saw between her grandparents.

She watched her dad in action on the farm, how he managed the agricultural venture, then watched him enter the business environment and negotiate with first the United Mine Workers and then the United Steelworkers Union. Again, a picture of contrast and diversity.

At one point in time 1,300 people were employed at the plant. Carol remembers walking through the foundry with her dad and watching him greet everyone by name. He would just as easily speak to someone on the production floor or say "Hi" to the floor supervisor and then walk right into the president's office for a conversation. She enjoyed watching the crews manufacture products. She says, "It is part of who I am to respect and love manufacturing. I appreciate the service industry and all the other industries where it's more of an exchange of ideas, but give me manufacturing—that's what appeals to me."

Carol adds, "It's taken a pandemic for our country to reflect on the value of goods and manufacturing and to reinvest in our infrastructure and our ability to recommit as a country to our basic manufacturing, our manufacturing base. It is the core of who we are as a country, and it is how we are going to maintain our leadership in the world."

At that young age, following her dad around the plant, Carol visualized her career path and that path was manufacturing. She says, "This is how I am going to make my living. This is where I'm going to be—it's manufacturing. I don't know what I'm going to manufacture or where I am going to work, but this is what I am going to do."

Carol credits Junior Achievement for helping her understand how to run a company. In school she attended evening sessions where students created a company, decided what products to sell, and assigned job titles and responsibilities for each role. The program taught the young people how to manage and be leaders. Everyone learned about stocks and each child was given shares of stock. They learned what it meant to have equity in a company. The groups not only had to create a product for sale, but they also had to figure out how to produce that product and then sell it.

Carol's group produced coat hangers. To this day both she and her parents still own a lot of those hangers. She says her parents were one of her group's best customers. Through the program she learned about costs and establishing a fair selling price, how to keep accounting records of goods sold, and the excitement of reaping the rewards when product was sold. At the end of the school year the company was liquidated. "It is the whole life cycle of a business," she says. "At that early age a lot of things gelled for me in terms of love of business, love of the industry, but I also kind of liked telling people what to do." Carol is still a big supporter of Junior Achievement.

Another experience that influenced her career choice was her participation in the band. In Carol style, she says, "It wasn't enough for me to be in the band. I had to be the drum major of the band." She discovered that being drum major required a unique skill set. For example, "activities required me to be able to influence other people, my peers, without having positional authority over them." In other words, "how to get this crazy group to march in the right direction and follow your lead when you're not paying them."

Carol discovered she liked this challenge of having no control over the band group yet still needing to influence and convince them to do what she wanted them to do.

She was inspired by these experiences. She had "a love for industry," and she was fascinated with "making something," which really started with her going to work with her dad. I wonder if he realizes how much he helped influence and guide her to love manufacturing.

Carol saw some of the downsides of the business world but was never dissuaded from pursuing manufacturing. Since her dad was responsible for negotiating employee contracts with the union and

High School Band Drum Major they lived in a small town, it

70

was impossible to completely separate his work from the family's personal life. She says she "saw the good and bad, ups and downs" during those negotiations so she wasn't naive about the more troublesome aspects of business.

Carol watched her dad, noting how he spoke to people and how he respected who they were and what they did at the foundry. She learned to "take the person as you find them, accept who they are, and make the best of it."

Something else Carol learned was trusting people until it's time not to trust them and giving people the benefit of the doubt. Learning these lessons and seeing them put into practice has really paid off for her in her career.

Bottom line, Carol is having fun at HarbisonWalker. "I am able to bring to bear all those core values, and I finally found a place and a group of people that also have the same set of values."

Carol had earned her master's degree and her law degree by the time she started at PPG. She had "aspirations of buying and selling companies, doing mergers and acquisitions," she says. "All of the fun stuff."

It might have been due to gender, but she felt fortunate to be surrounded by people who wanted to support her. At the time, it was not uncommon for her to be in a meeting surrounded by twenty to thirty men. Early in her career at PPG, she had several very influential managers take her under their wing and guide her. To be promoted in the company, they said she needed experience in sales and other areas within the company.

Finally, she realized that she was trying to be who everyone was telling her to be instead of who she was.

An example Carol gave me happened within a five-year period. Management's perception of her went from being too aggressive and a "bitch" to being perceived as a lightweight pushover. She had to stop and ask herself, "Who am I? Who is Carol Jackson?" It took time and self-reflection "to stop being the person I thought other people wanted me to be and start being who I knew I had to be in order to be good with me."

Carol said, "When women first got in the industry, we had to be like a man." You were already standing out when you used the ladies' room. You were one person, one woman and thirty guys."

She was in industrial sales at the time. Customers responded well to her. She was working with metal fabrication shops where it was not uncommon to see a *Playboy* bunny calendar on the wall. Restrooms for women were an afterthought. She tried to fit in and was successful. She wasn't afraid to get dirty. She was used to that from the farm.

On the job, working hard.

Some of her best memories were making calls with the tech service guys. It was the beginning of the consumer electronics coating business. PPG was selling paint to the applicators for consumer electronics companies such as Palm, Nokia, and Motorola. These companies specified the paint. The applicators/metal benders bought the paint and applied it to OEM specifications. They would start up the paint lines, which typically took thirty-six to forty hours. She remembers crawling around UV chambers in the middle of the night alongside the service guys just to be sure everyone knew she wasn't afraid to get involved. She wanted the guys to see that she would do what needed to be done to make the startup happen. This was a challenge for her, but she developed a reputation for being a hard worker. Customers loved her, and management credited her with those successes. She also says she got everyone's attention.

She had three degrees by that time and wanted to demonstrate that "not only was I good on paper, but I could actually get results." When people are successful, others start paying attention. Key managers started following her rise within the company, and she ended up having a lot of sponsors and great opportunities.

Every opportunity she was given, she generated the desired result. Carol is a big believer in "no matter how big the company, no matter how small, you have to live with the consequences of your decisions."

What started to happen is that Carol would be put in a position to create change and "you barely start to see results before they move you again." Carol says she can see how some people love this kind of challenge, but she also sees a disconnect in today's business environment. Management in some companies still has the "expectation that people are going to blindly do what you tell them to do." For example: "You need to move ten times in your career. You are going to do an expat assignment. You're going to go and do what we tell you to, and you will have a wonderful career." Carol admits she signed up for that initially.

She was in her rotation in procurement, part of the "do what we tell you to do—you need this experience," when Carol began to question what she really wanted to do with her career. She became "disillusioned with the way you had to run a business in a big, public company." Carol saw how many public companies continually made short-sighted and short-term decisions to meet quarterly expectations. She understood the process, shareholder value, not wanting to negatively affect stock prices, but she also recognized the impact these decisions had on the people and the processes within an organization. She was questioning if a big company was where she should be focusing.

Panel discussion at AISTech 2019.
(Photo courtesy of AIST archives)

Carol had given a lot of thought to the gender bias issue. When she came into the business, she was following in the footsteps of a few smart, capable women who came before her. One woman she admired was a coil and extrusion sales rep, and Carol says she finally retired after something like sixty years at the company. This woman started as a secretary and by the end of her career was indispensable and "basically drove the profitability of the coil and extrusion business for PPG." Carol remembers she was incredibly passionate about what she did. "So, it wasn't lost on me that I came in on the heels of pioneers like this woman. She opened the doors for women in sales, and some of the entry-level positions, had a successful career, and could have run the company."

Carol says she has respect for women who were the pioneers in the industry. When Carol started at PPG, the company was beginning to put diversity programs in place. Carol pushed back on this because she struggled early on with not wanting to be labeled a female. She just wanted to be given an opportunity to do the job and be recognized for doing it successfully. She acknowledged the reasoning behind these types of programs but struggled with the perception in the company that women were given jobs because they were women and not because they were the most qualified. She wanted it known she was given a job because she was the best candidate for the job, male or female.

Carol remembers speaking at a women's conference within the company and telling the audience that basically, "if you don't ask for something, don't expect it to be given to you. If you admire somebody, ask them for coffee, ask for the meeting—don't wait for it to be given to you because it won't." One of the managers approached her afterward and told her she had a good presentation but had offended some of the women in the audience. She remembers thinking that she had just told it like it was.

So, Carol struggled, as many of us did early in our careers. As she puts it, "How do you balance the reality of being a woman but not wanting a hand, not wanting special attention, or special help? I just want to do my job, do it well, and be given credit for the success."

Carol feels a lot of women have the perception that if you do a good job, you will automatically receive recognition. "You have to self-promote," she said. That is what she had to learn, and it is something "women still don't seem to understand."

I told Carol years ago, early in my career, I saw a little boy, maybe three years old. He was in the grocery cart with his dad. His father saw someone he recognized, and he came over to the grocery cart. He introduced his friend to his son. His son immediately held out his hand to shake the hand extended by his father's friend. It was at that moment I realized how hard I had been working to make my customers and co-workers feel comfortable with me. I also realized that as a woman it was hard to compete with men who had grown up with that mindset and training, what this little boy was experiencing at the age of three. Carol agrees that women didn't have that conditioning. But she sees this generation of young new hires coming into the business and "they don't see gender, they don't see cultural diversity; they just see the other person."

Through her career, Carol recognized that even though more women were hired through diversity programs, "biases were still there—they just went underground." Conversations that were previously more open and disparaging about women occurred less frequently, but that didn't mean the biases didn't exist. According to Carol, it wasn't only gender biases but age biases. Because she had excelled at every job she was given, she was promoted quickly, but then the "unwritten rule" kicked in. Within the company, "you couldn't be a director until you were thirty-five, you can't get to that level until you were forty." Again, it was another form of bias—a perception, a belief—that had no merit.

Fortunately, Carol feels this perception has also changed, "if for no other reason than you're going to lose really good people." That was what happened to her. She was fighting both age and gender biases.

One of the executives at PPG had left the company and gone to work for Carpenter. A year after his departure, he called Carol and offered her a great job in the bar, wire, and strip business managing the P&L. This is what Carol had wanted to do at PPG. "Don't give me sales, but not operations. Let me run the business."

Carol was excited. She says in retrospect her decision to leave PPG was the right one. But she did say she went from a big company to a smaller company. She worked hard and learned a lot. Carpenter had just bought Latrobe Steel and it was thought she would eventually move back to Pittsburgh and manage that operation. But while Carpenter was a big company in the steel industry, it had a small-company mentality and Carol had difficulty integrating into that mindset. In addition, she thought Carpenter was a healthy, well-run, and established business. While it was a great experience for her, she just didn't see how she could make a big difference and add value to the bottom line. She says, "There wasn't much to fix."

Carol had already left Carpenter when a headhunter from Pittsburgh contacted her about a job opportunity at HarbisonWalker (or ANH, which was the name of the company prior to Carol's joining it). Carol quickly realized she had the expertise HarbisonWalker needed in terms of experience, vision, and values. She says this is "why I am loving the life here at HWI. Harbison-Walker has been on an improvement trajectory for a number of years." She sees more opportunity and is pleased to be able to see the impact of the decisions and improvements that have been made thus far. Again, an opportunity she wasn't given earlier in her career.

It took this transition to HarbisonWalker for Carol to understand "where my personal value is, where my niche is, and it's just not maintaining a business." She says she is not a coaster. "That's just not my thing. I am a problem solver. I am always thinking about whether it's organizational, structural, or growth for the business, what can we do, what do we need to shift, adjust, change. I am a business improvement person. It took me fifteen years to realize that's more my thing. I have a mission and objective. It's also a slow burn because when I fix something it's a sustained fix. To do that, you must influence culture and people's belief systems, get them going in the same direction, which is often a departure from a big company." It was the same challenge she faced as a high school band drum major.

Something that Carol can do at HarbisonWalker that she couldn't do in the past is that her decisions are not short-term, knee-jerk reactions for the business. As she said earlier, "Short-term decisions are not sustainable. You need to implement a strategy, a plan, and give it time to work. Tweak it when you need to but do everything possible to make sure it is successful. When it is successful, make sure to congratulate the team and celebrate the win."

Where Carol sees she adds the most value at HWI is recognizing and understanding that to have sustained change, you need to articulate and identify what must happen and create an alignment for success. That means making sure your people are on board with the direction you want them to go. As Carol says, "People fundamentally need to believe in what you're saying can be done; they have to believe that it has to be done. And then you give them experiences to reinforce those belief systems and allow them to act against the given goal. That can take years. It's a slow burn."

HarbisonWalker has 180 years of history, a legacy of working with customers and getting the job done. The founders of this company worked with Andrew Carnegie and supplied refractory product for his steel production.

According to Carol, "Every business leader, in every generation, has an obligation to make things better, to make things more stable and more sustainable. We have to figure out a solution for recycling and reclaiming and getting to an economy where input equals output" in a true circular movement.

If you group together customer focus, ingenuity, investment, and automation with a belief in the industry and love for the industry, you are creating the new generation of manufacturing and commitment to the environment. "That is why I am here. It is what and why I do what I do."

**_e_ how you came to be asked to serve on the Board
ectors for Sentient Technologies—a company that is
involved in colors, flowers, and fragrances—and how is this
connected to the steel industry?**

Carol explains that her life and career goals included board service. "As I ascended to the C-Suite and had more engagement with board-level conversations, I realized that I had a passion for that governance" and examining how the company is performing and being run.

It is also helpful for her to have other board experiences as she progresses in her career. As she looks toward retirement at some point in time, she will become more active in her board service.

She says this particular opportunity came "out of the blue. They were looking at adding certain skill sets to their board." Carol's background in P&L, her leadership as a CEO, and her legal background were all reasons for asking her to serve on their board. "They do have a segment of their business which is industrial in nature, however. It was a safe way to learn more about a consumer-based business."

It is "well documented that once you get your first real public company board assignment then other offers will follow." A year later she received a call about another board opportunity and now sits on the board of AZZ Inc., an industrial metal coatings services provider. She also sees a push to have more women serving on boards and "more diversity in general on boards and in policy-making. This translates to having governance and driving philosophy at the highest levels."

She doesn't see this trend ending anytime soon.

What are you most proud of?

She is most proud of "what we are doing with this company at HWI. That story is not final yet, because there are some really great things still happening. Just from 2014 and then in 2017 when I became CEO to now. What we've accomplished. We are such a healthier, materially better company, because of a few things I have had the pleasure of leading. That is a source of pride."

Secondly, she adds, "when I am sitting on my porch in my retirement looking back on my career, it's actually more the people I've helped and seeing their careers advance that will mean the most. I get goosebumps when somebody that I've managed years ago calls and updates me on whatever they are doing and thanks me for something I did or said, something I made them do or feedback I gave them. Especially now, in a place where I am influencing so many people's lives and professions in a positive way, it is a great source of pride for me."

Carol talked about a concept in level five leadership. The concept was originally developed by Jim Collins, author of *Good to Great*. Its focus is the powerful mixture of personal humility and indomitable will in leading people. A concept called "force multiplication" combines the "power of numbers and alignment." When you combine these two aspects of your business, it can produce great results. That is what Carol is seeing at HarbisonWalker. "Being able to empower, enable, and inspire people to want to do something, to be better, strive to achieve a goal, and actually achieve it is the coolest thing for me and where I take the most pleasure."

How are you identifying future leaders at HarbisonWalker?

HarbisonWalker offers a leadership development program called LEAD (Leadership Excellence: Accelerate & Develop). Carol describes it as a "manager leadership development program for people in their mid-careers who have leadership potential and want to further their careers." To be accepted into the program, a candidate must meet certain criteria and be nominated by someone at the senior director level. The company also offers a career development program and career objectives for everyone. This includes both business and professional goals. Leaders and managers are supported and encouraged to have conversations about goals with their direct reports. This means the company needs good managers in place, so they have set up training and development programs for management.

As Carol says, "We now have a HarbisonWalker Academy that we are launching this year." This program "provides a catalog of educational opportunities in collaboration with online universities to provide additional training and development." Some of the program is formalized and some of the program is on an "ad hoc" basis, meaning that if an individual feels they need to understand how another department works, they will offer training to help that employee improve their performance.

Carol says, "Everything is metric-driven. We measure a lot around here, but that's how we get results." We metric the managers to make sure we hold them accountable for supporting and communicating with their direct reports and even those who are one step below their direct reports. In other words, the company is creating monthly and annual accountability for each employee. "We are tackling the concept of self-advancement," and that one size does not fit all.

The company recognizes that not everyone wants to manage or aspires to be promoted, but what HarbisonWalker does recognize and respect is that each employee wants to feel valued and challenged. "Our goal is to get our employees engaged in a way that makes them want to come back to work every day and be a valued contributor."

What are your thoughts about benefits?

Carol immediately talked about flexibility at work. This was after I saw a dog's tail wagging behind her. She had brought her dog to work that day.

She talked again about the concept of one size does not fit all, which is how most benefit packages are organized. "One of our core beliefs is we want to make HarbisonWalker a great place to work." She says the definition of that and how that came about as a goal "is based on the fact that our people were telling us that we wanted to bring our whole self to work." This conceptually means being authentic, acknowledging your personality, and bringing your hopes, dreams, and fears with you, even if they don't seem relevant to work.

In order to accomplish this they formed an engagement task force that focused on employee engagement feedback on many things, including health benefits and wellness programs. This team of alternating volunteers shares feedback and makes annual recommendations to management on what HarbisonWalker has to do to stay relevant and be a competitive employer in the world." For example, the company not only offers maternity leave, but paternity leave, as well.

As a result of a diverse workforce, they also implemented employee input policies to accommodate their "voices" in response to COVID-19. When possible, accommodations were made to allow people to work from home. It is a combination of all the above that put HarbisonWalker's turnover numbers in the single digits, a metric the company monitors daily.

Retention rates for hourly employees remain one of the biggest challenges for the acquisition team at HarbisonWalker, but it is something management is watching closely. Another area the company is monitoring is retirements. With retirements comes the loss of critical process knowledge within the operation, which is "knowledge they need to use to train the next generation." Management is working closely with this group

"Short-term decisions are not sustainable. You need to implement a strategy, a plan, and give it time to work."

of employees, offering incentives when they can, to convince them to stay and work a little longer. This allows critical knowledge to transfer to successors. Even with automation, Carol says there is still a lot of knowledge that is not quickly or easily automated, and that alone is a big challenge right now and for the foreseeable future. Some answers, she says, "you just can't find in a book."

What is your definition of success?

"No regrets," Carol says.

"The way I view success is through goal achievement, which is hollow if you compromise safety and quality." She adds that one of her beliefs is "you never leave a man behind."

Part of success for Carol at Harbison Walker is that "bad seeds weed themselves out in a culture that's as strong as ours. We either succeed together or fail together."

What is your definition of failure?

Failure is "not trying. This is where leadership really can influence a culture," Carol says. "There was a time in the company when it was not okay to fail." The downside of that approach is "it creates an overly conservative attitude, a paralysis to get anything done because you're not one hundred percent certain of success.

"Part of the tools we put in place is fast failure. Identify what can go wrong, how do you mitigate the downside, and leaders must empower their people to fail. It's okay to fail, but pick yourself up, dust yourself off, and learn from it. Do better next time." Carol says that is what you need to do when you are weaning people away from a culture where there are negative consequences for failure. Instead, "you have to create a safe space for failures."

Carol says that the approach and thought process around failure is scalable. "You aren't going to put an experimental product in a ladle because people could die. So critical applications are exempt from this because of the severity of the outcomes. The same goes for the aerospace industry. If you have institutional process control, that is where the discipline, focus, and opportunities for failure can allow for innovation and progress in a safe way."

What are your thoughts about leading versus managing?

"I tend to use a battle philosophy. The leader is the person out front, first in the battle and the last one to leave the battlefield. That for me is leadership. As it relates to people, *a leader's job is to get out of the way*. In other words, make sure you provide your people with everything they need to succeed and let them run with it. Make sure you have the right people in the right places with the right tools. We use diagnostic tools and profile assessments and have identified what leadership means to us."

Carol says "It means you are clearing the roadblocks and ensuring that you are truly force multiplying as an organization, then get the heck out of the way. It is the ability to see the bigger picture and ability to project. Balance, levelheadedness, stability, strength, ethics, and the ability to inspire our definition of leadership. Leadership is also humility. It is also about setting the tone and modeling behaviors and values. Leadership is the hardest work, in my view, because it requires you to be quiet a lot, and actually listen and be there for your people."

Lastly she says "Good leaders can be good managers; I am not so convinced good managers are necessarily good leaders. Managing is a little more tactical in nature."

What is your definition of happiness?

Carol says "my dog." In a recent conversation she said, "It's like one hundred percent love and dedication, and all they want is to be fed and in return they give you so much joy."

Do you notice any differences between how women approach their jobs versus men?

"Women bring an emotional intelligence, a feminine touch. It's a sensitivity too. Women are just generally more in tune with all of the aspects of a subject or in the decision-making process." Of course, she has seen women with no emotional intelligence at all.

Carol talked about the popular TV show *Madam Secretary*. In one of the episodes, a character in the show comments that the secretary of state (played by a woman) reacted very emotionally to a situation. The secretary explains that when a man gets emotional, he is viewed as putting emphasis on something, or he is particularly passionate about a subject. When a woman reacts in the same way, she's regarded as too emotional; it's considered unprofessional.

Carol says, "I think women who are confident in the workplace are some of the best, most engaged people because they are not afraid to express themselves—and generally speaking, they are often more charismatic and engaging."

"Women have a hard time in the workplace," Carol says. She decided early on not to have children. Her mom would tell her that she didn't have a maternal instinct, which Carol begrudgingly acknowledges, but she says she does with her dog.

I disagree with her because of what she has shared with me during this interview. She is very concerned with her employees and doing the right thing. She involves her management and employees in decision-making that ultimately affects their work experiences and their desire to come to work and help the company succeed. That is what a family does. Your idea of maternal is not about one or two babies, but thousands of employees and how you can bring them all to the table to talk, respecting one another while creating an atmosphere of success and equity.

Carol says, "I couldn't have done both extraordinarily well. My life is about work and that is the legacy I am leaving." She says, "You can make whatever choice you want to make, but just acknowledge there will be consequences to those choices." She "knew men who spent 90 percent of their time traveling. They lost years with their kids. There are always consequences, and sometimes people don't understand what they have sacrificed and given up until it is too late. You can never go back; you can only go forward."

* * *

"The life/work balance is different for everybody." As a business leader, how willing are you to give people the ability to be flexible when they need to be? The culture that Carol has created with her team at HarbisonWalker is "that we care about employees. Every single one of our employees matters and what they do matters. They do add value, so we value our people. This is what is going to distinguish us in the future.

"Part of the reason I am living this culture is because my career opened my eyes to the challenges folks have." Carol is grateful for what she has, and with a nod to the lessons she learned from her father, who looked his employees in the eye, knew many of them by name, and respected what they did. She wants to not only give back to her company but to the employees as well.

* * *

Do you have any quotes or stories that are particularly meaningful to you or that motivate you?

"Become a student of this business. You're smart, but you don't know everything."

Carol added, "In light of the changing world, whether it is a life event or because you question things, I now firmly believe: Do what you love and love what you do. And, if you don't, then change it."

* * *

You have brought a lot of light into the business world and HarbisonWalker. Thank you, Carol.

About HarbisonWalker International

With more than 150 years of industry leadership and global recognition, HarbisonWalker International is the largest refractory products and services supplier in the United States. Headquartered in Pittsburgh, Pennsylvania, the company's international network spans North America, Europe, and Asia, with eighteen manufacturing plants, twenty global sourcing centers, and technology facilities in both the United States and China. Serving virtually every major industry that requires refractory solutions to enhance production and protect assets, HWI is consistently recognized for its talented experts, industry firsts, and intensely driven excellence.

To learn more visit, thinkhwi.com.

Chapter Five

Roxanne Brown

United Steel Workers Union, Washington DC
International Vice President At-Large

She Stands on the Shoulders of Her Great-grandmother

In 1967, Roxanne's great-grandmother had recently emigrated from Jamaica and was living in White Plains, New York, hoping to make a new life for herself. She was employed as a domestic worker before joining the staff at New York Presbyterian Hospital, where she became a dietary aide.

Gradually the matriarchs of Roxanne's family immigrated to White Plains. Her great-grandmother and grandmother were the first in the family to immigrate to the United States. They were followed by aunts, cousins, and then Roxanne's mother and Roxanne, who was two years old when her mother brought her to this country.

Her extended family, which included great-aunts as well, occupied two apartments in the same building. Some of them worked two jobs seven days a week to make ends meet. This is how she grew up, Roxanne says, "raised by women. I come from a family of mostly women." Her husband says she was raised by what he calls "The Generals," because of the strength, guidance, and determination of these women. Her father and the bulk of her father's family stayed in Jamaica, and many remain there.

While her grandmother still resides in the apartment she grew up in, the rest of her family "moved on from that building and had families of their own."

Roxanne's goal was to finish college and go to law school. She was enrolled at Howard University in Washington, D.C., but ran out of money and was heartbroken that she had to leave college when she was nineteen. Her boyfriend at the time, who would later become her husband, was attending George Washington University. He gave her a business card for a temp agency. She made contact, and the next day the agency sent her to the Steelworkers Union office in Washington, D.C. She has worked there for twenty-three years.

Roxanne started as a receptionist and says, "The rest is history." She worked in a clerical position for many years until one of her mentors realized she was capable of more. She benefited from a newly created progression in the union for clerical staff who outperformed their responsibilities. From her clerical job, she was promoted to resource technician and continued to build on her progression. "I never in a million years expected to be an officer of this union when I walked through that door in 1999."

I asked Roxanne what her responsibilities were as vice president at large. She says her predecessor, a Canadian who retired last year, was the very first vice president at large for the union and was the very first female officer and executive board member of the union. Roxanne was promoted to fill her position, which includes oversight of the union's atomic membership employed at the Department of Energy Cold War legacy sites across the United States. Roxanne, who is based in Washington, D.C. accepted a few additional responsibilities. Much of what she has done for the union is steeped in policy. Her responsibilities now include overseeing the atomic sector as well as oversight of the union's legislative, policy, and political work.

Roxanne says the past few years have been "hectic." 2020 was the first year she had to run a political program since it was an election year within the union. She says the union organized a membership engagement program called "Your Union, Your Voice." As part of that campaign, they organized more than 170 town hall meetings around the country to talk with their members about the core values of the union and learn about the issues that were priorities for USW members such as access to health care, retirement security, and the right to organize and collectively bargain.

After the election, the union launched a major campaign focused on infrastructure to help push for the passage of a significant infrastructure bill. "We supply

"Leaders support and work along-side the people in an organization, not over them."

America" was a nine-month membership engagement and policy initiative. The campaign included legislative work on Capitol Hill, writing labor-management letters to policymakers on the critical products and services USW members supply, and a multi-state bus tour in August 2021 to drive the passage of the bill in November 2021.

Years ago, when the idea of Roxanne potentially becoming an officer of the union first started, she asked the union's former legislative director, who is also a mentor, what his thoughts were. "It's not about you," he said. "It's about what you having that position means for the union and for women who look like you and for the movement." Roxanne agrees with this assessment, but she adds that it is also "challenging the notion of what a steelworker is and what we are supposed to look like and sound like."

Was anyone in your family a member of a union?

Roxanne says her great-aunt was a nurse's aide and worked at the Westchester Medical Center until she retired. Her aunt was a union member of the American Federation of State, County and Municipal Employees (AFSCME.) She grew up going to the union picnics "not really understanding what the union stood for."

Why did you choose to stay and work at the union?

Roxanne's first day at the USW coincided with the first day of a union-run legislative intern program. The program brought together local union members from across the country and across all the union's sectors for three months to learn about policy and lobbying. At the completion of the program, USW members earned twelve credits at the National Labor College.

Roxanne says she fell in love on that first day with the authenticity she saw this group of USW members bring with them to DC. Here they were, all very much out of their day-to-day elements, but as Roxanne says, "they brought themselves into the Washington, D.C. culture, into our office space, and it was so amazing. I got to see firsthand who our membership was, and I just fell in love. Every year I couldn't wait to meet the new group of interns." At that time, the USW Washinton, D.C. office was also organizing a lot of rallies on Capitol Hill around trade policy, so Roxanne was able to see the union in action on many levels.

"Had I not had the opportunity to interact with our members on day one, and then through the internship program interact with our membership on a continual basis, my path would have been much different," she says. "I wanted to finish college, go to law school, and become a lawyer. This may sound cheesy: my connection to the membership immediately connected me to the work of this union, and it lit a fire in my belly."

Roxanne says one of the aspects of their membership that she loves is that "they bring their authenticity." I asked her what she meant by that. She says when the union goes to lobby on the Hill, and all the "policy-speak" is being thrown around about health care, retirement security, health, trade issues, and other pressing subjects, what their membership does is remind the legislators and the politicians how these issues affect them directly. For example, "one of the members may describe how 'my son has been fighting for his life the last two years from leukemia,' and how a certain bill or clause in the bill will impact the family. Or 'let me tell you what the economic impact in our community will be if two hundred people are laid off.' Those are the authentic stories, the plain-spoken truth that people in Washington, D.C., who live in a bubble, need to hear."

That is why we try to bring our membership in to lobby, to testify before the International Trade Commission (ITC) or testify on Capitol Hill on these issues because "you need to bring that kind of truth-telling into the policy arena."

What have you found most challenging in your career?

When she first started with the union, there were few women in leadership positions. Now, many of the departments of the union are led by women, and there are now two women on USW's executive board including Roxanne.

Roxanne can honestly say she worked her way up the career ladder at the USW, much like a laborer will work up to a foreman's position, supervisor, manager, or executive, which is the American way. She didn't come into the union with a college or law degree, so she has had some insecurity around this as she has moved up through the union ranks. Most of her interactions on the Hill with politicians and lobbyists are with people who have their law degrees.

As Roxanne has grown into her various roles with the

union, she has come to value what she brings to the table. She knows she deserves to be at the table and has proven she can hold her own place in this space with the lobbyists and politicians.

Another challenge that Roxanne understands is that even though she is very comfortable walking into any room with their membership, she is "still aware that some of their members may not like that it's someone who looks like me walking into the room."

She is also aware that some may not feel as compelled to have the union engaged in social and racial justice efforts such as Black Lives Matter. Roxanne says, "As a social justice organization in our own right, it's our responsibility to be allies to other like-minded social justice movements."

An additional challenge is balancing being a mother of a four-year-old and traveling. She says historically with mostly men in leadership positions in the union, issues revolving around childcare or taking care of aging parents were not something they commonly had to navigate because of traditional support systems at home. "That is not my dynamic," Roxanne says. "My husband is a physical therapist, and his hours vary. My family is in New York and his family is in Philadelphia, so scheduling is really a challenge." But many women in our union both on staff and among our membership face these same challenges. This is one of the reasons it's important to have women in leadership, as we are in tune with these types of struggles and are inclined to try to create the infrastructure and flexibilities on the job to help manage these responsibilities.

Women in the union membership have also shared with Roxanne that at the local level they want to become more involved in the leadership of the local unions but sometimes struggle with breaking through the traditional leadership. That's why programs like the union's Women of Steel are so essential to training rank and file members in the USW to actively engage with their union and pursue leadership roles.

Can you remember an instance, situation, or meeting where you just reacted and then realized that yes you could command a place in this big space we are talking about in Washington, D.C.?

Roxanne remembers speaking at a gathering in Pittsburgh in 2019. "Afterwards I was speaking with a group of members about their frustrations with the proposed Green New Deal and how they felt left out and unseen. They felt they were going to be left behind by these policies. This conversation was a microcosm of the larger conversations I have in Washington, D.C. about avoiding the unintended consequences of climate policy, particularly as it relates to manufacturing and energy workers. It allowed me to talk to our members about the work our union does on behalf of them on this very issue in Washington, D.C. and how we're making sure their voices are being heard."

"It's important that the membership realizes their industry will continue to change and evolve, because that is the nature of the industry, but they need to know we're fighting like hell to make sure there is going to be a place and a future for them. Those types of conversations are the moments where I pinch myself. Do I really get to do this? Is this really my job? I actually get to fight on behalf of these folks."

What has been most gratifying for you?

Roxanne says, "Securing wins." She knows that's cliché. "I don't even mean big wins; for me the victories are big and small. We just had a victory on this multi-employer pension issue. Our union played a leading role in helping to get that bill passed in Congress and signed by the president. Millions of retirees in a variety of industries were going to be impacted if this bill was not passed.

What are you most proud of?

"We're not afraid to do what's unpopular." Probably one of the best examples of this, she says, concerns the energy, environment space. The union "engaged in energy and environmental policies going all the way back to the inception of the Clean Air Act. We've done much of this work through a health and safety lens. Our members are the first line of defense when it comes to toxins and pollutants and potential disasters at facilities. So much of our work on these issues has been about keeping our members and their communities safe, as well as helping the industries they work for be more globally competitive."

Roxanne says the USW held the first conference of any industrial union on clean air in the 1960s. We ultimately ended up playing a key role in writing and helping to shape the original Clean Air Act in the 1960s and the following amendments in the 1990s. "Protecting the environment was unpopular with the steel industry at the time, but it was doing the right thing for our membership."

She also mentioned the work the USW is doing on climate change, an issue the union has focused on since 1990. In 1990, the USW called climate change "the biggest threat to our world and our children's world. We have been working on these efforts since then and now."

Roxanne says, "Today so much of our work is around making sure that sectors like steel, aluminum, cement, oil, paper, glass, and the other primary industries our members are in don't just survive the transition to a clean energy economy, but thrive. All these industries and so many more helped build our economy and our infrastructure systems. They are just as critical to building our future."

What have you learned about yourself?

I learned, "I am tougher than I knew. This job has probably made me extra tough because we've had to fight some challenging battles on behalf of our membership. We are extremely diverse in term of the sectors we represent; we say we're cradle to grave because we represent health care workers and gravediggers and so much in between. These different interests require us to serve our members in a variety of ways and within varying arenas."

Her work at the USW has also challenged her definition of family. Meeting the interns that first day of work over twenty-three years ago and then over the years interacting with not only the USW membership, but also with the USW staff, really catapulted her definition of family to another level. Her partnership with the union has extended her family way beyond anything she could have ever imagined.

Is there anything else that is unique about you and what you bring to the table?

Roxanne says, "Being a black, immigrant woman, my life experience is different. Being able to bring that perspective and experience to the work of the union is unique and has been beneficial."

She also says that being a mom is unique as well. For many years the executive leadership was comprised of men. Being able to bring a mom's perspective and being a successful role model to the younger staff demonstrates that women are advancing in the ranks of the leadership of the union.

Lastly, Roxanne's extensive policy experience is another aspect of her career that makes her unique. So much of the work of the union from collective bargaining to organizing to the viability of domestic industry rests on the ability of the union to engage effectively with policymakers. Her experience in this space has proven beneficial to her work on behalf of USW members.

What is your definition of success?

"Constantly moving the goalpost forward."

What is a pivotal experience for you?

Her first pivotal experience was her first day of work at the USW and meeting the interns. The second pivotal experience was one that required a difficult conversation with a group of her labor colleagues from other unions. It was on an issue where it was thought USW did not have much skin in the game.

Roxanne discovered why she had a place at the table that day and her perspective around this issue garnered respect from her colleagues, even if it did not garner everyone's agreement. She says, "When I feel uncertain about a path forward in the policy space, I pull from history."

Are there any stories or quotes that motivate you?

What motivates and drives Roxanne is her expanded family. Family is always a grounding force for her. Being an immigrant and Jamaican, growing up in New York is her identity and important to her. Roxanne says, "I stand on the shoulders of my great-grandmother. The women in my family refer to ourselves as the 'Findlay women' in honor of my grandmother. It speaks to the strength and stubborn determination that courses through all of us. It is the tie that binds us."

Best advice anyone ever gave you?

"Always tell the truth."

What would you like people to know about you?

"I love our union and our membership deeply. I will always do my best on behalf of them."

What is your definition of leaders versus managers?

"Leaders support and work alongside the people in an organization, not over them. I firmly believe in a team approach where no job is above anyone on the team, including the leader. Leaders also need to be willing to listen and create the space for their staff to share ideas and suggestions. Our union is filled to the brim with such talented people. It would do us and our membership a great disservice if we didn't tap these talents and abilities to move the union forward."

Roxanne describes herself as "a hands-on leader." She feels a leader should be able to lend a hand in any way to help her team.

* * *

As we end our discussion, which includes Roxanne's daughter telling me she has a playdate that afternoon and a wiggly tooth, Roxanne says her "daughter is the promise of why she came to this country. The struggles my great-grandmother, grandmother, and my relatives overcame are the same types of struggles our members have today. When I do this work, it is not just on behalf of our membership, but it really is on behalf of my family and the struggles we had coming to this country. I see my role, as working to help improve the standard of living and opportunities for workers across this country. I cannot emphasize how damn proud I am of that."

And it all started with her great-grandmother's dream of wanting to come to this country to create a better life for her family.

Thank you, Roxanne.

About United Steelworkers

The United Steelworkers (USW) represents 850,000 workers employed in metals, mining, pulp and paper, rubber, chemicals, glass, auto supply, and the energy-producing industries, along with a growing number of workers in health care, public sector, higher education, tech, and service occupations.

To learn more, visit usw.org

CHAPTER SIX

Eva Dillon

ArcelorMittal Dofasco
Steelmaking Technology Business Unit Manager

A Five-Year Business Plan at the Age of Twelve!

E va was one of six children. She had four brothers and a sister. Her family lived in North York, a suburb of Toronto, Ontario, Canada. And yes, she created a five-year business plan for herself at the age of twelve. Her plan included joining the Royal Canadian Air Cadets at twelve, working through the cadet program, and applying for a glider pilot's scholarship at fifteen.

Her two older brothers had joined the Canadian Air Cadets and Eva followed that same path. She asked one of her brothers what she had to do to qualify for the glider pilot's license scholarship. He told her she had to be the best. She needed to take a test, which was a certain percentage of your

Sergeant Eva Dillon receiving Most Outstanding Cadet award in 1991 as a member of the Royal Canadian Air Cadets.

score; have an interview; receive a recommendation from the commanding officer; and sell raffle tickets as a fundraiser for the cadets.

Eva made sure she had perfect attendance at the cadet squadron. She participated in all their parades and even went on extra camping trips. Whatever activity the cadets sponsored she attended. Each cadet was responsible for selling two books of raffle tickets as a fundraiser. Eva sold fifty-three. She didn't particularly like selling tickets, but she figured it was a numbers game and she was fearless about asking people to purchase tickets. After receiving the glider pilot's scholarship, she went away for the summer and received her license. She was only sixteen.

The culmination of her five-year plan was to earn her private pilot's license by the time she was seventeen. Her five-year plan was well executed until three weeks after she received her glider pilot's license. Eva's father died in a private plane crash. Eva was devastated. She'd lost her father and she'd lost the airplane that she was hoping to fly as a pilot.

She looked at her five-year plan and had a choice to make. Her friends and family did not know what she would do. Would she let her dream of getting her private pilot's license go or would she follow through? She chose to return to the cadets and received her private pilot's license the following summer.

To this day, Eva loves to fly. She is still a glider pilot. She has her instructor's rating and has taught dozens of young people how to fly gliders and taken hundreds of people on their first introductory flight. Although she loves flying, Eva was never interested in becoming a commercial or military pilot.

Eva was educated in publicly funded Catholic schools.

She was student council president and a member of the debate team. Everyone knew who she was in high school. Senior year she was even elected "Student of the Year."

She followed her sister into engineering at Queen's University in Kingston, Ontario, Canada. Materials and metallurgical engineering was the smallest department in the engineering program. However, when Eva attended information night and saw the instructors pouring miniature ingots and "some cool things with shape memory, alloys, and polymers," she was hooked, and thought this field would provide her with good career opportunities.

She gained experience in metallurgical engineering by working in a gold mine in northern Ontario one summer and in a coal mine the following summer. She says she would have been happy to work in the mining industry when she graduated and even applied to several mining companies and a few construction companies when she graduated.

After graduation, Dofasco in Hamilton, Ontario (now ArcelorMittal Dofasco) offered her a position in metallurgical technical investigations. It was an assignment many engineers considered a "dream job" because she was working in a lab with sophisticated

Eva became a champion of continuous improvement methodology and worked with operators in the plant on many improvement teams.

equipment. Dofasco had an excellent reputation, and the company was only an hour away from home.

Her family had a background in the metals industry. In the 1950s, her grandfather invented the Dillon triple-level floating point vibrating screen for the mines, sugar refineries, quarries, etc. Prior to his death, her father had traveled and installed the screens at different mining locations.

In her new position, Eva was using an electron microscope and searching for defects in steel equipment failures. She equates her investigative work to CSI, a popular TV show about the work of forensic investigators.

Dofasco had a rotation program. After two years in the lab, she began working in various departments in galvanizing. In the finishing area, a new automated

Eva next to a Dillon triple-level floating point vibrating screen during her summer job at the David Bell Gold Mine (1998)

surface inspection system had been installed. She was one of the first engineers to start analyzing statistical data from the equipment. The company formed a new department to analyze the data, which would enable the mill to develop better quality control measures, minimize customer issues, and reduce internal down-grades. Eva was part of this group for several years.

Since most of the projects were related to steel-making, she had the opportunity to get to know the department. They started asking for her help with special steelmaking projects.

At Dofasco, individuals often participate in special assignments and sometimes the special assignment can be a "coaching" position. This is considered a supervisory position. They promoted Eva to coach for the customer service product development group in steelmaking. She spent several years in that role, which she found interesting. Not only did this group handle internal quality issues, they also conducted trials for advanced high-strength steels, and worked with a cross-functional team to ensure trials were not only successful in the caster, but downstream as well. She says it was a very technical group, mainly engineers, but people from operations would often transfer into the group.

Eva "became a champion of continuous improve-ment methodology and had the opportunity to work on many improvement teams with operators in the plant." The team would use the methodology to check, act, and identify the reasons for failures or problems and brainstorm and develop countermeasures they could implement themselves.

She also became involved in a maintenance set-up project in the EAF (electric arc furnace). A consultant had taught her a concept Toyota had developed in the 1960s. It was called a single-minute exchange of die (SMED) methodology. This methodology helped streamline maintenance downtime. Basically, the concept was if there was work inside the shutdown period that didn't need to be done, don't do it. If there is work that can be done ahead of the shutdown to simplify, improve, and lessen downtime, then do it.

One of the pipefitters approached her and said they weren't accustomed to that mindset. Once the team understood how their actions could impact downtime, they suggested a flood of projects that could help in this effort. The group ended up shaving off two hours of downtime monthly, at a time when downtime cost the company three hundred dollars a minute. No one had ever shared that information with them. This insight had a monumental impact on the employees and operators, and they began to provide suggestions and solutions not only for the melt shop but across the entire mill. Some suggestions also improved safety, an ongoing issue in the steel industry and in manufacturing.

Eva had her first son shortly after that project, effectively ending her time in steelmaking. Since she knew she wanted to have several children, she agreed to work on a special assignment with the corporate strategy team. At that time, management was evaluating the company from the highest level, looking at the direction the company was going, where the industry was headed, and what Dofasco needed to do to prepare for the future.

After her second maternity leave, her former boss promoted her to utilities technology business unit manager, two levels below a vice president level. She was responsible for the technology department and all the engineering and technical staff for the utilities department. This included the boiler houses with three turbo generators, water treatment plants, an acid regeneration plant, and a central trades group that refurbishes equipment on site. Eva was in this role for over three years and has recently returned to steelmaking as the technology business unit manager.

Eva likes the collaboration involved in the job. She has adopted the company's slogan: "Our product is steel. Our strength is people." During her initial interview with Dofasco, Eva was asked why the company should hire her. She quoted that slogan and said, "That's me." She also told them she "wanted to be part of that strength and work with their people and achieve great things."

Eva is a problem solver. She has always enjoyed discovering a problem that someone was experiencing in the mill and solving it on a collaborative basis. Oftentimes, she had a suggestion or solution that not only saved the company money but also increased safety. Eva has saved the company millions of dollars during her career with Dofasco and enables others to do the same.

At her team meetings, she would often bring blackberry upside-down cake, made from blackberries that came from her own backyard bushes, which everyone enjoyed. As it turned out, one of the electricians on the team had a secret talent too. He was Mr. "Cake Boss" in his own right. He started making cakes for his children's birthday parties and the hobby expanded from there. He volunteered to make a special cake for the team, which was dotted with a miniature marzipan team member in an orange mill jacket. That same team member was an illustrator, and he did cartoons of the team members. The team came together, not only to solve issues and make improvements at the mill. They came together by sharing and celebrating their outside talents and interests too, and had fun.

Earlier in her career, she remembers one afternoon when she had finished her work for the week. She decided to take a walk through the mill and chat with some of the operators. It happened to be the "tea shift" in the pulpit that day so they made her a cup of tea and asked what she needed. She told them she didn't need anything. "What type of person would I be if I only came to talk with you when I needed something?" The guys laughed. One of the pulpit operators was so appreciative that Eva had reached out to them that he said, "I am going to teach you a secret," and he shared his secret to make large spangled galvanize.

How did Dofasco respond to the COVID-19 crisis?

Her response surprised me. Eva said the company already had a pandemic plan in place in the event of a breakout of SARS. The plan included onsite accommodations for employees such as housing, food, medical, etc. When COVID-19 started, cases in Hamilton, Ontario, were contained, but other mills were reporting ten times more cases than Hamilton.

Eva complimented her pandemic team for implementing procedures to keep everyone as safe as possible. With young children, Eva was apprehensive about going into the plant and bringing the virus home with her.

Her husband, who is a coach in the pickling lines, was onsite at the mill while she worked remotely.

What have been some of your biggest challenges in your career?

Eva says that her pregnancy turned out to be a challenging time. To get to her office she had to walk through the plant, past the BOF shop, and up three flights of stairs. Due to the dust and the electromagnetic current in that area of the mill, and the unknown effects of this exposure on reproductive health, the safety department told her not to use her office.

She laughs recalling how on the very day she told her manager she was expecting, another female employee had come into his office to tell him she was expecting too.

During her pregnancy, her job title was "Improvement Coach." In this position, she was assigned new capital projects as well as large maintenance projects. Fortunately, she had two new employees she trained to oversee the projects while she was on maternity leave.

Another area that Eva found challenging was articulating and developing her leadership style over the years. Company-sponsored leadership training classes helped her learn about herself and how to adapt going forward.

Dofasco sends all new employees through team-building exercises to identify their personality types and Eva was identified as a "driver." Drivers are one of four personality types (drivers, analyticals, amiables, and expressives) and are typically fact-based extroverts. One of the coaching programs she attended was set up as a high-performance session. These sessions were designed to help the company determine if employees had the capability to be a leader in the company and to learn about the company's leadership expectations. They used Myers-Briggs, and the data showed that the current leadership in the company were primarily "analytic," or technology-oriented managers. Eva thought if she was going to be promoted, she needed to find a way to be viewed as more analytical by upper management. So, Eva enrolled in a six-sigma black belt course to help with this transition.

Eva began to do statistical projects with steelmaking defects and established herself as an "analytical" within the company. But in one of those damned-if-you-do, damned-if-you-don't moments, one coach at the company told her she was a bit of a robot and suggested she ought to let people see her more human side. She realized she needed to be more amiable because she wasn't trying to teach operators advanced statistics. She was showing operators how to solve problems and motivate their teams to want to solve problems on their own.

In one of her leadership courses, it recommended asking for feedback from her co-workers. Eva contacted operators on the teams she was championing and asked them what personality type they thought she was. To her surprise, not one of the operators identified her as an "analytical." Most of the operators said she was "amiable or a driver." However, if you asked her general manager at the time what Eva's personality type is, he would say she is "super analytical, almost a Vulcan" (the logical alien species in *Star Trek*). For Eva, it was understanding what technique works best with the people you are working with, but also how important perception was in this evaluation. Even though her manager thought she was a Vulcan, the operators thought she was amiable.

The third challenge for her was recognizing that for the first fourteen years of her career, she was able to analyze data and use statistical analysis to problem solve even if she was unfamiliar with the subject. She would consult with experts in a subject area and ask if her conclusions were correct based on the analysis. In her most recent promotion she has realized she is not using her analytical and statistical analysis skills as often.

A leadership course she had enrolled in said most people reach a certain management level using the same problem solving or creative methodology that they have always used. What the class was teaching was that you need to continually develop and diversify new skill sets in your toolbox because old skill sets may not get you promoted to the next level.

Eva is experimenting with different methodologies and approaches. She gave me an example. In the past she would not have thought to use her social connections to help her accomplish something. "Apparently using the social levers is a common practice," so now she has no problem leveraging her social connections to do this.

This course also taught her about perception. The

question in the class was: What percentage of employees do you think are promoted based on hard work, via networking, or through personal branding? Most women say 80-90 percent is based on hard work and the other categories have minimal percentages. However, men will typically rate networking and personal branding at 70 percent and hard work at 10 percent. A lot of professional men and women feel that working hard will get you noticed and promoted. They don't focus on networking or promoting a personal brand. Eva coaches her employees, both men and women, to realize they need to create an authentic personal brand that reflects who they are. It is the reason why some people are promoted when there are other individuals more qualified.

How many women work at Dofasco?

Roughly 12 percent of Dofasco employees are women. Eva observes numerous women in technology, metallurgy, and the commercial group. Her former college roommate is a general manager and her current boss. Her boss was the first woman technology general manager for manufacturing technology.

The female operations manager in her department started her career about ten years before Eva. At the time of our interview, one of her female employees who had been with the company for forty-one years was now the senior technical employee in the company. Both women have worked with the first female vice president of technology and vice president of manufacturing at Dofasco.

When Eva became the customer service coach, she was the first female coach in steelmaking. When she moved over to the electric furnace to be improvement coach, she was the first woman to be the coach in that area, and she is now the first female business unit manager in steelmaking. (Although other areas in primary, including coke making, and utilities, have had female business unit managers as well.)

Eva notes that the majority of law students and medical students in Canada are women. There are a lot of women in chemical engineering and to a lesser extent materials engineering. By the 1990s, only 5 percent of professional engineers were women, while roughly 20 percent of the engineering students were women.

Eva told me in the 1930s and 1940s, Dofasco hired dozens of women to physically inspect tin plate before shipping it to the customer. The women wore gloves and even had a special lunchroom since it was considered shift work. Fast forward to the 1990s when there were massive layoffs and shutdowns in the industry. When the industry began to call people back to work after the layoffs, they were offered whatever job was available at the time. As a result, many women ended up in new and exciting positions that they might never have thought of doing.

The first female engineer that Dofasco hired in the melt shop, Jane Wood, asked Eva to go with her to the department retirement banquet she attended every year, to meet her old manager. Jane said he was the one who decided that Dofasco should hire a woman in the department. He felt the unit would be a better team if they had the benefit of a woman's perspective. Jane wanted her previous manager to know that even though she had moved into another project management role in the company, he had been right to hire her and wanted to introduce him to Eva, who was now the coach in the same area. Eva said that you know someone can be the first person to accomplish this or that, but there is usually someone behind the scenes or in the forefront that decides it is time for change.

Just prior to our interview, Mr. Mittal, CEO of Arcelor-Mittal, made an announcement concerning diversity and inclusion. He announced a new target to increase the number of women in leadership positions at the company. He recognizes that if you want to attract top talent you can't just look at 50 percent of your population.

* * *

I mentioned to Eva that her career focused on team building, mentoring, and empowering employees. When everyone began working at home during COVID-19, she said she had enough work for her team to cover the first few weeks. She didn't know how engaged people would remain after that or how much opportunity for training would be available. She came up with an idea that management and the executive team approved.

She called it "Training Tuesday." The goal was for peers to teach peers about an area in which they were an expert. Sessions were recorded so that if someone could not attend, they could listen at a later time. Eva selected a talented engineer as the first presenter. He oriented his program toward "non-electrical engineers." His program included quizzes as well as graphics from popular TV shows. It was creative, fun, and educational. One of the VPs at the company listened in and was so impressed he said the program should continue. The first wave of "Training Tuesdays" lasted for six months. When I interviewed Eva an average of one hundred people were tuning in to the training sessions each week.

Realizing that one of the training sessions followed International Women's Day, she asked ten women from the company to spend five minutes discussing their careers. Her goal was to give the attendees an opportunity to learn about different job opportunities that were available throughout the company. Eva had witnessed women with technical degrees in the company accepting positions in other departments and making incredible contributions they would not have been able to make without a technical background. The panel members were selected for this special session and more than seven hundred employees joined the session. Half the listeners were women, but the information applied to young men as well. Eva received tremendous positive feedback. Listeners were inspired to learn about the different career paths that were available in the company.

She then shared with me a story that ended in a discussion about diversity and inclusion. Eva said one year had been difficult for the company but everyone in the department had done very well. Management wanted to have T-shirts printed for the three hundred department employees. Everyone thought this was a good idea until she heard what the slogan was. She could see how the slogan's message could be misconstrued and prove embarrassing. The slogan had been discussed and agreed upon by a group of male managers and one female administrator, who had not offered any negative feedback about the slogan. Eva raised her concerns with several of the coaches, who, after hearing Eva's logic, agreed with her. She was voted the one to call the manager in charge of the project and discuss the issue. After listening to her concerns, the manager agreed with her. Additional attempts for a new slogan were discussed, but in the end, a decision was made to simply include the company logo and department name on the shirtsleeve of each T-shirt.

Eva's point in telling me this story was that the group of managers thought that by having a woman participate in the meeting they had "checked the box." She feels when it comes to diversity and inclusion that it isn't a matter of "checking the box." Just because you have a woman in the room, or at the table, won't always guarantee that the right decision will be made.

Her point is if you are going to hire someone, see that they fit the values of the group. You have to ask if the group is going to value their opinions and input. If you simply hire women to "check the box" so you can tell your stakeholders or your board that the company is diversifying the workforce, the question becomes not how many women managers were hired, but rather a year, two years, five years later, how many have stayed and what impact did they have within the operation.

Did you ever have anyone approach you inappropriately?

Once in a standing-room-only meeting, one of the older guys, rather than giving her his chair, motioned for her to sit on his lap. Others who did not know Eva were insulted by this gesture and found it offensive. One of them stood up and offered her his seat and apologized for the other employee's behavior.

Some of the women who had joined the company ten years before Eva said the crews were very protective. One time, a contractor from outside the plant whistled at one of the women employees. When the operators heard his, they had the contractor up against the wall and told him that you don't treat our people that way.

Eva sees a big brother mentality, a family mentality in the mill. She sees family traditions from people who have had fathers, uncles, brothers, and grandfathers who have worked at the company over the years.

What is your definition of success?

"It is the feeling you get when you've accomplished things that you want to get done." Eva has an existential outlook on life. She enjoys her work and feels it will guide her on a path going forward. She has never been someone who aspires to certain management levels by a certain age. That isn't how she thinks. She says success should really be about achieving your goals but also understanding why you want to do those things.

Eva feels she has had a lot of successes in her life. She had her pilot's license before she could drive a car. She prepared and implemented a five-year business plan at the age of twelve, which included joining the Canadian Air Cadets, becoming a glider pilot, getting her private pilot's license, and later receiving her instructor's rating.

She says her team at work celebrates their successes. They usually not only surpass their goals but "we usually knock it out of the park." She wants the path to that success to be enjoyable and makes sure that group members savor their achievements and enjoy going home at night to share their successes with their families.

What is your definition of failure?

Eva thinks failure "is not so much about not achieving the results you're hoping for, but more about not achieving those results in the manner in which you're hoping to achieve them." Not only does she challenge her team to complete a project, or an objective, but Eva analyzes how they accomplished the task. She feels fortunate to work for a company that supports a culture that focuses not only on results, but on the methodology used to achieve those results. Even the company's HR department has gone on record asserting that how you achieve results is as important as the results themselves. Failure can also mean using methodology or rewarding someone for using a methodology that is punitive to obtain results.

What is your definition of happiness?

"Happiness is seeing the smiles on my sons' faces." They are six and four.

What can we do to attract more women into the industry?

Eva says several women in her engineering class majored in engineering because of attending a very cool summer camp at Queens University when they were twelve or thirteen. The program, called "Science Quest," had been going on for twenty-five years and the university had an outreach program that always sent a male and a female engineer into the classrooms to encourage both girls and boys to become engineers.

Even during her summer internship at the gold mine, there were fewer than ten women, out of a thousand workers, employed at the mine. Eva says many people still assume that she works in an administrative position at the company.

She wants young women to know that there are women at Dofasco who are working hard and making real bottom-line contributions at the plant. Women are working in numerous roles across primary steelmaking (coke making, blast furnaces, utilities) and throughout the finishing mills, enjoying their jobs and excelling in careers.

What are the most important things you have learned about yourself?

Eva believes that learning to be more flexible and trying different approaches with her team and management was important. When she was younger, she would drive results by either doing a lot of the work herself or assigning tasks to people whom she knew would complete the job. Now, she sees the benefits of delegating and mentoring not only to get results, but to help improve everyone's performance. She sees the benefits of understanding her team's strengths and weaknesses and how important it is to "leave behind a workforce that is well trained and motivated and has the skill sets they need to be successful."

What is unique about being a woman in this industry?

"Look at the ratio of men to women," she says; "that in itself is unique." She was at an electric furnace conference in Phoenix, Arizona, and was the only representative from her company. One of the men at the conference asked her to join their group for dinner one night. There were nine men and Eva. She noticed an older couple watching them throughout the evening. On their way out they said, "We have been watching you interact with your table of men. We think you're doing great."

* * *

Even in her flying club, out of twenty instructors, only two are women. The flying club would go on week-long flying excursions and the rule was "No women." They changed the rules for Eva. The men, who were twenty to thirty years older, asked her husband if he minded her going and he told them, "You know my wife is an engineer and a pilot. I'm pretty sure she can handle old guys like you." She is just as interested in the other pilots seeing her as a pilot as she is others seeing her as one of the leaders at Dofasco and not as a woman leader or woman on the team.

Another experience she shared with me was when she was at military camp getting her pilot's license. She had brothers and attended all-girls schools, so she was accustomed to participating in class and being called on by the teachers. At military camp, 80 percent of the class was male and the boys were physically bigger than Eva. When the teacher asked a question, the boys overpowered her, and she felt lost in the crowd. Eventually after the third day of not being seen or called on, she quit raising her hand to answer questions.

The instructor liked to target students who were underachievers or not paying attention, so one day he asked a question. The boys were waving their arms in an attempt to answer the question but the teacher called on Eva. The question dealt with relative humidity and moisture in the atmosphere. She responded quickly with a perfect textbook answer, which impressed the instructor. When one of the boys tried to add to her answer the instructor silenced him immediately. The boy glared at Eva and the instructor said, "You can't add a single thing to her answer that would make it any better; her answer was perfect," and he gave Eva an apologetic acknowledgment, letting her know he had indeed misjudged her.

During the final test, she was uncertain about an answer to one of the questions. She ended up changing her answer. If she had not changed her answer, she would have received 100 percent. The instructor told her, "Never change your answer, Eva. Always go with your gut and that is my advice to you." He went on to serve as a fighter pilot in the United States military. The experience of wanting to be heard and acknowledged, and being drowned out and overpowered by a bunch of aggressive male teenagers, has stayed with her. She says that women who haven't grown up with brothers and know how they talk, and what they talk about, can be intimidated by this behavior.

She remembers realizing she needed something to

wear to her job interview at Dofasco after she graduated. She told the sales clerk that she needed something neutral because she was going to be touring a
steel mill and added, "I can't dress like Erin Brockovich
and not expect people to look."

* * *

What do you do for yourself to get away from the testosterone in your life?

This just isn't a priority for her in her life. She says
even her hobbies involve men. At one time she was
riding motorcycles with her husband and his friends.

She talked about the day they offered to provide a
mill tour for the Association of Women in the Metals
Industries (AWMI) chapter. The company provided
women guides for the groups that would be touring
the BOF furnace and the caster. When they got to the
pulpit in the caster, there were twenty women in the
pulpit, two operators, and the coach who had been the
leader of this area for many years and an employee in
the mill since the 1970s. The coach saw this group of
women, got a big smile on his face, and the women
started asking good questions about the process, etc.
Several days later he saw Eva and she asked him, "Do
you remember the way you felt the other day when you
walked into the pulpit and noticed all of the women
from AWMI who were here for the tour?" He nodded
and Eva said, "That's what it's like every day for me,
just in reverse." He laughed and said he "should have
gotten a job at a lipstick factory or something instead
of steel."

Eva said, "I go to work every day and there are ten or thirty men in the pulpit doing whatever, and I am asking them questions and they're asking me questions. We're working together and having fun." But there are always more men than women, particularly in operations.

For the week after our interview, Eva had planned a Zoom call with a group of nine-year-old Girl Guides/Girl Scouts. She was going to talk to them about centrifugal force and how it affects an airplane. She was also going to tell them that even though there aren't a lot of women at the steel mill, the girls can choose to be an engineer or a pilot or whatever interests them.

Eva worries that her sons may feel shortchanged because she doesn't always have the time to spend with them. When the boys were home during the COVID-19 lockdown, at 4:30 p.m. they would come and find her and tell her it wasn't work time anymore. She tells them, "When you are the manager, you don't have a quitting time until all your work is done."

I asked Eva what ambitions she has for herself.

She says, "Ambition is not so much that I see a certain position I want to attain. It is more about continuing to develop transferable skills and having more opportunities to build upon my previous experiences."

She remembers reading a book written by an admiral and the strategies he used to improve morale on a ship whose crew was known for bad attitudes and poor work practices. Utilizing the successful strategies he used on the ship, he selected five or six companies and analyzed their performance and conducted case studies for each company. One of the women interviewed from the study was discussing her job aspirations. She wanted to do meaningful work, contribute to the success of the company, and develop skills that would help her grow professionally and personally. Eva said there were no tangibles, no timelines, for attaining a specific management level within a certain number of years. Her aspirations were wide-ranging in the sense that it was more about the essence of her work and the value she wanted to create.

Eva related to this woman's perspective and started using similar terminology in her performance reviews. Her boss criticized her and said it was "too high level" and if she wanted to become a manager, she had to articulate exactly what she wanted. She added the following sentence to her review: "Yes, I want to be a manager and the next thing you know, I was a manager."

Eva says, "It is not so much about the endpoint; it's about the journey and getting there. Right now, my entire career, I've enjoyed the journey. I certainly didn't predict I would be in this seat."

What are you most proud of?

She says, "Being true to myself and doing and honoring the things that are important to me and keeping them close."

Getting her pilot's license, she says, was not that difficult, but earning the scholarship to get the pilot's license proved more challenging. She is proud she identified goals she wanted to accomplish and followed through to make them happen. When she became interested in engineering, she went into engineering even though some of the professors didn't treat female students with the same respect they treated the male students.

Eva says there will always be people who think you shouldn't be there, or feel you aren't qualified to be there. She hasn't had those problems. When she needed to take time off to have her two sons, the company supported her. When COVID-19 hit, and her kids were home and she wanted to take time off to be with them, she did. She didn't feel pressured not to do that, as other people she knows who work in different industries felt. "You need to avoid feeling pressured, and do what makes you happy." If you choose to give up a lot of things you want to do in your life for a perceived end result and that end result doesn't happen, where are you in your life?

Do you feel you have been adequately compensated in your career?

Eva says "yes." Dofasco has a rigid compensation program that she feels prevents wage discrepancies based on gender. She feels women are not vocal enough when they discover a discrepancy in salaries and encourages them to bring discrepancies to management's attention.

Is there a quote or story that inspires you?

Eva doesn't know who said the following but her number one slogan is: "The only place that success comes before work is in the dictionary."

She tells people to "be genuine and be themselves. If you stay true to your values and objectives, you won't ever find yourself in a position where you ask, 'How did I ever get myself into this situation that I'm miserable?'"

What is your reputation among your co-workers?

At Dofasco they have a program at the plant called "Thanks a Ton." It gives people an opportunity to acknowledge a co-worker for something they've done. A worker who reported to Eva was transferred to another department and gave her a "Thanks a Ton." He said she was the strictest boss he had worked for, and she was firm but fair. Eva was very pleased. "Firm, Fair, and Friendly" was the simple leadership model she had learned as an air cadet.

She prides herself on being approachable and supportive, and in her career development evaluations she has been complimented on providing valuable feedback about career options and other areas for improvement. She did say there is a balance you need to maintain between professionalism and being too friendly.

※ ※ ※

We ended our conversation talking about how some men don't understand that while some women are motivated to become a manager, an executive, or a president, not all women are here to "take over." Eva said, "Many women want to be a part of something important, something that is bigger than we are as individuals. We want to continue to build and redefine this industry and contribute to its prosperity and relevance."

You are flying high, Eva. Thank you.

About ArcelorMittal

ArcelorMittal employs approximately 168,000 employees in 60 countries. Flagship locations like ArcelorMittal Dofasco play a vital role in inventing smarter steels for a better world. Founded in 1912, ArcelorMittal Dofasco is Hamilton's largest private sector employer with nearly 5,000 employees. Each year, the company ships 4.5 million net tons of high-quality flat carbon steel. And they partner with the top automotive, energy, packaging, and construction brands to develop lighter, stronger, and more sustainable products—from cans to cars.

To learn more, visit dofasco.arcelormittal.com

CHAPTER SEVEN

Elena Petrášková, LL.M

U.S. *Steel Košice*
Vice President, Subsidiaries and General Counsel

Here Comes the Judge!

E lena says it was a well-known fact among her law school friends that she would "never, ever work for a steel company." Steel mills were dirty places, and she wanted nothing to do with that environment. Instead, Elena wanted to be a judge. She liked to make decisions and to make decisions for other people.

She had tremendous respect for her late father, who had spent his career in the steel industry at what is now U.S. Steel Košice, but was previously VSZ a.s. Her father worked in maintenance in the blast furnace. He was called upon regularly to help create solutions to problematic maintenance issues and was one of the "go-to" people in his department. Elena is very proud of this.

Her mother, who died some years ago, was a crane operator in the finishing end of the mill. When I told her you don't see

"We are promoting the steel industry as a business for the future."

133

many women crane operators in the United States, she said it is not unusual to see a woman crane operator at her facility.

Over the years she saw how hard her mother and father worked in this industry and the commitment and pride they had in doing their jobs well. Elena inherited her parents' work ethic.

After law school, Elena was waiting for an interview to become a judge in the court system. As it turned out, the interview with the justice department was delayed for several months. Fate, as it worked out, had interceded.

Knowing she was waiting for her interview, one of her classmates contacted her asking for a favor. He had found a new job and needed to find and train a replacement.

Because he was a very good friend, she committed to working at the steel mill for three months, although she told everyone she was waiting for an interview for the judgeship, and she had no long-term intention to work for a steel company.

Thirty years later Elena is still with the same steel company.

When she told her first boss at the steel mill that she was only at the company temporarily and that she would never work in the steel industry, her boss took her disdain for steel mills as a challenge. He committed to showing her what the steel industry was all about and the opportunities that were available to her. He put a lot of time and thought into educating her about steel production, management, and how the business changes daily.

Three months later when she got the call for the interview to become a judge, she turned down the appointment. "And I am still here," she says. I asked her what prompted her decision to abandon the judicial system for the steel industry. Elena realized working for the steel company allowed her to use her skills and talents in many ways. She saw herself negotiating contracts with customers, and suppliers. The work was challenging and she could visualize herself negotiating with the utilities and helping the company's represen-tatives negotiate with the trade unions. Elena says, "It was really about someone showing you the beauty of this business. It was very interesting, and I was lucky I had a tutor who helped me, and my parents."

For Elena, all these opportunities to influence and negotiate on behalf of the company and the employees contributed to changing her mind about her career choice. She realized she could better utilize her skill sets in business than by "going to the court and just talking." She also recognized there was an opportunity to work with the government on issues surrounding the industry. She found she began to like the people she was working with. Elena realized she had been privileged to have the right people at the right time appear in her life to support her and help her make decisions.

Because she was educated and trained as a litigation and later corporate lawyer, Elena said this background helped her "understand our relationships with suppli-ers and customers, as well as the whole steel business."

Three years after the Velvet Revolution, a nation-wide protest movement took place in Czechoslovakia from November to December 1989, ending forty years of communist rule in the country. Everything in the country was changing and business was conducted in a different way. "It was a very dynamic period."

Elena started to work as a corporate lawyer in 1993 at the steel mill's headquarters. At that time the company employed 17,000 people and was the largest steel company in Slovakia.

In the transition from a state-owned company to a privately owned company, the company went through various phases of restructuring. Management realized that with 162 subsidiaries, they needed a different way to oversee the operations and began to consolidate the businesses. Though the company was still partially owned by the government, the new owners received support from the current political party in power. However, in 1998, the company began having difficulties meeting their financial obligations and recognized they needed another investor. The banks had another idea and named Elena's boss as president of the company. He was to begin the restructuring process and prepare the company for sale to a new investor.

On November 24, 2000, U.S. Steel purchased the company and took over the assets. During this time, Elena was working in the legal department. This was a big transaction and proved very challenging for the entire legal team tasked with organizing not only the subsidiaries but the overall business. By that time, Elena had worked for the state-owned steel company that had partially transitioned to a private company, for eight years. She had the opportunity during this time to see the pluses and minuses of being in that business environment. At one point, two thousand people at the mill were scheduled to be terminated because the mill didn't have the money to pay their salaries.

Due to all the negotiations during the purchase of the mill by U.S. Steel, Elena had developed good working relationships with the upper management at the new company. During this time, she was privy to critical high-level decisions, and this experience gave her another layer of knowledge about decision-making at the executive level. She also saw how the business environment was changing not only for their steel company but for other industries as well.

Elena says she is an admitted "workaholic." "I like to work, and I love my work." She tells her two children, a thirty-two-year-old son and a twenty-five-year-old daughter, that "you have to love your job, you have to love your school." If you like what you are doing, "you can handle the difficult times."

U.S. Steel's management recognized Elena's commitment to the transition. The acquisition of a formerly state-owned enterprise by a private company presented a huge learning curve for both entities. Her boss was the general counsel for U.S. Steel, and the two parties relied on interpreters to translate. Negotiators on both sides had to acknowledge and work through communication issues and navigate different legal systems. The last and biggest hurdle for Elena was that she didn't speak English, which made explaining situations and moving forward even more challenging.

In 2005, her supervisors recommended that Elena and her family move to Pittsburgh for one year so she could work in the legal department at U.S. Steel's corporate headquarters. She said this was a frustrating work experience for her because of the language barrier. In addition, her legal education and experience practicing law in Czechoslovakia was quite different than American law. Even with these barriers, Elena said they successfully concluded several international agreements and negotiations.

Her daughter, who was in fourth grade when they moved to Pittsburgh, was challenged because she didn't know the language. Her teachers were very supportive. Elena remembers a school assignment where her daughter had to speak to the class about her native country and the government. The presentation was a success and boosted her daughter's self-confidence.

Eventually her children became so acclimated to school they were sorry to leave their friends in Pittsburgh when Elena and her family returned to Slovakia a year later. Elena continued working in the law department. She became involved in the Slovakian version of AIST, called the Metallurgy, Geology and Mining Industry Association and became the first woman vice president in the history of the association.

"You have to rely on the people who know the equipment, who know the procedures. I know a couple of people to call when there is a problem. They are not university-educated people, but they run this company and we rely on them."

One year after her return to Slovakia, U.S. Steel management asked if she and her family would move back to Pittsburgh for a longer assignment. One of the reasons was that U.S. Steel wanted her to get her law degree in Pittsburgh. She says the differences in the legal philosophies between Slovakia and American law were significant. But Elena also felt she needed to understand the United States legal system and "what American lawyers are thinking."

138

She and her family returned to Pittsburgh. Her children were fortunate to go to the same schools they had attended previously and were reacquainted with many of the same friends they had met before.

Her husband had been supportive throughout this time. His support allowed her to concentrate on working full-time, while spending her weekends in the law library and going to law school at night. Through an agreement with the director of the Center for International Legal Education (CILE) and the dean of the iaw school, Elena earned her law degree in two years. The concentrated timeframe was a challenge, she admitted, but she did it.

Elena was committed. She learned to speak English. She now had her American law degree too. During the recession in the United States in 2008, U.S. Steel was forced to close facilities in the States and Canada. When the Canadian government objected to the closing of the mill in Hamilton, Ontario, it was the combination of both her degrees and her legal prowess, along with the legal team at U.S. Steel, that finally enabled U.S. Steel to close its facility in Canada.

In 2010, Elena started working in U.S. Steel's government affairs office in Washington, D.C. She was still working with the legal office in Slovakia because the country was now part of the EU and that transition involved changes in legislation.

Finally, management decided it was time for Elena to go back to Slovakia, although some individuals felt she should stay and continue to work in Washington, D.C. and push U.S. Steel's interests in the United States. She accepted a promotion to vice president of the subsidiaries in Slovakia, which employed 2,100 workers. Within the subsidiaries were businesses that produced refractories and provided refractory services, security for the plant, laboratory services, and packaging.

At that time, she controlled $130M Euros of business. She was no longer practicing law; she was responsible for the overall business. She told management, "I am a lawyer. I am not an economist." Her boss told her they had confidence in her promotion because she was familiar with the mill and the business. She realized she knew the business because she had been utilizing her legal expertise to represent the subsidiaries for a long time. She realized she knew the people at these different companies, and how they thought. Elana was the first Slovak woman in the history of the Slovak steel company to become a corporate executive.

Despite the offer of the promotion, she didn't accept immediately. She realized this was a huge opportunity and would be a lot of responsibility, which she has never taken lightly. She reviewed the organizational structure as it was outlined. She wanted to know who was in charge and who she would be working with. After three days of wrestling with the decision, she accepted.

Some individuals thought she would stay in Washington, D.C. as a lobbyist, which many considered the "dream job." But at the end of the day, Elena realized she wouldn't have any real responsibility in that position.

In Elena fashion she started to learn more about the subsidiaries and what they did in terms of the refractory business, finishing and shipping, the intricacies of the chemistry lab, how to negotiate with each company, and about the collective labor agreements. Then in March 2011, there was an injury. She had to weigh in on that investigation because, as she says, "I was responsible."

She says that now she may be called in the middle of the night if there is an emergency or an accident. "It's different to be a lawyer, and it's different to be just totally responsible as a manager."

She has been in this position since 2011. More responsibilities have been added. She is now in charge of everything related to the power plant. She oversees supplies, production, and now distribution. She manages procurement of electricity and natural gas on the open market and oversees the legal department.

In 2013, the mill in Slovakia celebrated the fiftieth anniversary of the blast furnaces. Even though her father is deceased, Elena was proud they recognized him during that commemoration. They said while he wasn't the manager, he was the man they called when they had a problem that needed to be fixed.

Over the years, Elena has learned, "You have people around you, and they don't have to be managers, they don't have to be the president of the operation. You have to rely on the people who know the equipment, who know the procedures. I can name a couple of people who I know to call when there is a problem. They are not university-educated people, but they are the people who run this company and we can rely on them." A real life lesson.

She said something I have heard and experienced over the years: "Each year is different." This industry may be old in years, but it is still sensitive to politics, environment, weather, business cycles, imports, interest rates, the economy, and outside economies, and yet with all those variables, companies still invest in the steel industry. What does that say about the power and influence of this industry on our economy and in this country?

How have you dealt with COVID-19 at your location?

Elena said that dealing with COVID-19 has probably been the biggest challenge of her career. She is frustrated dealing with a situation that is out of her control, particularly when she is one of the senior management team responsible for 10,000 employees. At the time of our interview only 58 percent of the employees had been vaccinated, and all employees need to show they had been vaccinated or else they were tested. She says she has been very strict about enforcing rules. But as she realizes, it is hard to social distance in a pulpit and in other areas of the mill, so this has also been a challenge, especially when Elena has known people who have died from COVID-19.

What are you trying to do to increase the number of women who work in your company?

Elena says when she started with the company in 1992 women worked in HR, accounting, and finance, but there were no women in a director position or in top management. In terms of production, the only women were in support roles in quality control.

Elena had commented that her mother was a crane operator in the finishing area in the mill. She says there are quite few women crane operators in this area because there is a consensus in management that women are more focused and more precise about where they are stocking inventory.

Right now, Elena says two women are in top management. About 30 percent of the general managers are women. Women managers are also in R&D and in procurement. Elena sees a big improvement in women being promoted not because of quotas but because they are qualified for those positions. She sees women being accepted in these managerial roles, which is also important. Concerted efforts are being made to attract women into the steel industry through initiatives in high schools, universities, and the local technical university. "We are promoting the steel industry as a business for the future."

Elena says the company is also strongly promoting the industry as a major recycler, reflecting a concern for the environment and decarbonization.

The company supports events sponsored by the Women's Inclusion Network. This includes monthly online programs for all employees and focuses on topics such as business, economics, environment, energy, and health issues for women. The company sees the benefits of connecting employees' work or professional lives with their personal lives. Some other areas of discussion include ethics in both professional and personal lives, and discussions about European versus American approaches to the environment. Combined monthly sessions with U.S. Steel in North America have attracted more than 650 employees to online presentations.

What have you learned about yourself?

She says she is capable of learning to do a lot of different things. "I need to stay open-minded." For example, she felt challenged when she was put in charge of procurement for energy when she had no background in this area. She realizes she doesn't have to know everything in detail but can learn and rely on the experts in her organization.

Elena says she is inspired by a quote by Margaret Thatcher, former prime minister of the United Kingdom. "If you want something said, ask a man; if you want something done, ask a woman."

She goes on to say, "Don't be shy to present yourself and to speak out loud." She says her female colleagues are not shy, and in fact are quite vocal in expressing their opinions. Elena makes an interesting analogy. She says in some cases women have been discouraged by men in business from expressing their opinions. As a result of that bullying, women become hesitant and insecure about their thoughts and opinions. However, she has noticed, "If you are a mother and something comes up with your children, immediately we change and we are the lions, we are strong women, because we are fighting for our kids."

Elena tries to be creative with solutions and ideas. She wants to find the best person for the job. She also supports giving people second chances. Her colleagues say she is stricter than her male counterparts. But as she says, "I am responsible for the power plant and if I shut down the power plant, I shut down the whole company and the surrounding city, as the company supplies heat and steam to the city through the power plant."

What is your definition of success?
Elena has a lot of definitions of success. Sometimes

success is to be the vice president or a manager, but not exclusively because promotions are not always successful. Success can be simply doing a good job or being good at what you are doing. She admires people in the mill who are not lawyers but are brilliant at fixing things and keeping equipment and machinery working, much like her father did. Success can be something small you do for someone to make them happy or something you do for yourself to make you happy. Successful people aren't just the people you see on TV or on a screen in a movie.

What is your definition of failure?

Sometimes if we don't achieve our goals, it doesn't mean you've intentionally failed. There are often outside influences that can affect outcomes over which you have no control. Elena says her definition of failure is when you have done something deliberately to hurt someone or purposefully cause someone else to fail.

What is your definition of happiness?

Her definition of happiness is seeing her husband and children smiling. Her dog makes her happy. Seeing her neighbors makes her happy. To experience a beautiful day is happiness. She is happy when she can support people, not necessarily financially, but by providing advice that makes a situation or experience better.

What is your reputation at the company and in your community?

Elena says she doesn't know. She does know co-workers will often ask to be part of her projects and teams. People in the company will ask her advice. She has been a vice president for more than ten years, so she is recognized in her city of 250,000 people. The media often seek her opinion on subjects pertaining to the steel industry.

What have been some of your biggest challenges?

One of her biggest challenges was in 1998 when the company didn't know if they were going to be able to keep the mill going. That was a very difficult time for everyone. Her biggest challenge is with decarbonization, which is a huge issue for the company right now. Another challenge was moving to Pittsburgh and attending law school while she was working full-time and not fluent in English. Elena also mentioned accepting the vice president position and concentrating on management versus the law.

What would you like people to know about you?

She wants people to not be afraid to take advantage of opportunities that are presented to them. She uses the example of when U.S. Steel management gave her the opportunity to become a manager. She says people around you will be willing to support you when you take advantage of an opportunity. It is important that you not only accept help and support when it is given, but that you help and support others. She is currently working with a non-profit organization and is tutoring students from an orphanage. She says, "Giving from your heart is important."

What is your definition of a leader?

Her definition of a leader is "a person that people follow naturally." A leader also leads by example and that means supporting the team, because leaders don't operate independently; they are dependent on people supporting them. Leaders "need to listen" and need to be "capable of changing their opinions." A leader doesn't impose their opinion on the team. She says while there are lots of managers there are not many leaders.

Elena considers herself a leader and that people will follow her. Others have told her, "She is a natural leader of the people."

What are your visions for the company?

Elena sees a lot of transition at the company over the next ten years. While the mill is still dependent on BF furnaces the company will be installing electric arc furnaces. With decarbonization the mill will be reducing emissions and providing a cleaner work environment. The global utility sector is currently facing pressure due to the lack of availability of natural gas and electricity along with inflated prices of both commodities. This situation is seriously impacting costs and profit margins throughout the EU.

Elena is not sure she would like to be president of the company. She feels she has enough responsibility where she is right now as vice president.

How do you make sure that men and women are compensated equally at your company in terms of wages and benefits?

She says that all jobs in the mills are assigned a certain wage. Performance, not gender, is the only differentiation in determining promotions. Maternity leave is six months to three years. Each year Elena sees more men taking advantage of parental leave. She has heard the men brag about being home and doing the baking, cooking, housekeeping, and caring for the children.

Years ago, one of Elena's managers wanted to take paternity leave after he and his wife had a baby. Elena thought the other male managers would make fun of his request, but the response was quite the opposite. The managers quickly decided how to divide their co-workers' responsibilities for six months until he returned. She was very impressed with their response.

She believes it's important for the company to make sure that employees on maternity leave or paternity leave are kept informed as to what is happening in their jobs, departments, and the company so they don't feel alienated and uninformed when they return.

What are you doing to attract young people into the company?

Four or five years ago the company began to offer paid student internships. Each department, whether it is production or administrative, has one or two student interns who work twenty hours a week over one or two semesters. Students undertake special assignments and can work in different departments. Elena is making sure these students have the same opportunity to experience what she did when her first boss took her under his wing and taught her how the business functioned. Elena sees this as a win/win situation. The students discover if they have an interest in the business and the company can see if the students would fit into the culture of the company.

* * *

Not a bad story for a woman who wanted to be a judge.

Thank you, Elena.

About U. S. Steel Košice

U. S. Steel Košice is an integrated steel mill in Slovakia with more than fifty years of tradition. The facility produces 4.5M metric tons of steel annually and employs almost 11,000 people.

To learn more, visit usske.sk or ussteel.com

Chapter Eight

Shaina Huntington

TMS International
Manager, Marketing & Engineering

"I don't really keep a notch on the belt for the wins. I take a stripe on my back for the losses."

S haina Huntington is a force to be reckoned with. The contracts that she and her team negotiate can total $500M, numbers that affect the bottom line of any company's P&L statement. After working weeks and months on a contract of this magnitude, it would be disheartening for either side to lose, but if she does, Shaina goes back to review what the company quoted and digs deep to find out what they could have done differently. She says losses lead to wins and wins are always sweet. Shaina has had a lot of wins.

Shaina grew up in Boise, Idaho. As she says, "No steel industry in the state but a lot of farming." Her father is a builder, so she is comfortable around

"When people feel valued, their performance is positively impacted, profitability is impacted, and the return is exponential."

construction and admits to becoming 'one of the guys in a workspace.' I have always found it much easier to get along with the guys. They are easier to work *with* and be *around*."

Shaina has a master's degree in business administration and a bachelor of science in applied management, both from Grand Canyon University. "I went from farming to steelmaking and never regretted it." She had experience in manufacturing prior to starting at TMS as a forecast analyst. She was hired through a headhunter, by the CEO and president, Ray Kalouche. Ray builds his team with the premise that varying ideas and different thought processes can evolve when you encourage people with different cultures and backgrounds to work together.

Shaina was given more responsibility and opportunity to prove herself as TMS grew over the years. This included visiting worksites and steel mills. She liked putting on her steel-toed boots. The hook came the day she saw her first electric arc furnace in action. She was awestruck and told herself, "I want more of this."

She says, "The world would stop turning had it not been for the steel industry, for infrastructure, for innovation, for everything steel provides in society." She still finds the industry amazing. The more she learns, the more she appreciates the part she is playing in the industry and the "powers that keep it going."

She knew she had the president's support before she started but that support never changed. She is grateful that all of TMS' management values the *people aspect* of the business, particularly encouraging everyone to speak up and participate, not only in the discussion phase but in decision-making. To further support these diversity efforts, Shaina encourages the company to continue to be a sponsor of the Association for Women in Metals Industry, (AWMI) and and she encourages women in her company to join and participate in this organization.

Out of roughly ninety global sites, TMS has only a handful of women in executive positions. Shaina is one of those few. In operations and on the site level there are another half dozen women in middle management. Shaina recognizes that the company has a way to go before they have the diversification that CEO and President Kalouche aspires to create.

After less than five years, Shaina was promoted to manager of marketing and engineering. She oversees project development and contract acquisitions, and she makes certain the company understands the customers' expectations and that site operations are following through on the service expectations of the customer. She and the local operating teams continually search for opportunities for value-added services for current customer contracts. Shaina is also involved in building and maintaining customer relationships at the corporate level with some of the company's largest customers.

* * *

What is the impact you have on profitability in the company?

When TMS receives an RFP, it is Shaina's responsibility to complete the financial analysis, and to coordinate with the operating team to make sure they have the correct assets for the job and the appropriate staffing to provide the service level TMS is known for. As she says, "Any profit or loss is all on my pen." To put this in perspective, some of the RFP bids are potentially $500M contracts. A mistake or losing a bid greatly impacts the bottom line of the company. Her most challenging position in the company thus far is the one she has right now.

Are there any other skills that you have that would benefit the company?

The more Shaina is challenged, the more she realizes what she is capable of. You don't realize what you are capable of until a manager says, "I think you would be great in this area, or project or position, and let's give it a try." She continues to learn things about herself.

Where do you think the disconnect is for women in middle management advancing to executive management?

She feels some women have been in their positions for so many years that they are uncomfortable challenging themselves to change. Others may not see the value in moving up the ladder. Lastly, she says there are a lot of women who could come in at the executive level, but they don't have a construction background or understand heavy equipment or onsite operations. She feels it is such a niche in terms of skills and not many women have this area of expertise. "If those women exist, they are highly sought after—a unicorn."

Would you want to go into operations management to broaden your understanding of the business?

In fact, she turned down an opportunity to do this. She didn't want to butt heads with the "good ol' boys" who had been in their positions for many years and wouldn't take direction from a woman, someone they didn't know and hadn't worked with. Although she is both headstrong and vocal, she felt she could be more successful where she is right now. She feels you need to consider who you are working with and what level of acceptance you are going to get, particularly if you haven't worked your way up. In this case, as a leader/operator. Shaina says TMS has great women managers who have worked their way up in this environment, whereas she would have just been inserted into an area where she was unknown and would be expecting the crews to adhere to her management style and level of governance.

What impact have mentors had in your career at TMS?

She enthusiastically gives credit to a handful of strong men who have stood by her. She admits she wouldn't be where she is today, and in the position she is in, if this group hadn't challenged her. Because of this, supervisors and other management in the company have recognized her talents and said, "We trust your analysis and what you contribute to the company." A senior VP of marketing told the president of TMS that he expected Shaina to take over his accounts when he retired "and do a better job." She was astounded and can think of no greater compliment. She ended by saying, "I wouldn't have the joy and sense of success I have had it not been for these mentors."

There are no formal mentoring programs for women in place at TMS currently, although it has been discussed.

What personal challenges have you had while you have been working with the company?

One former leader made it clear to her that she was not good enough to be doing what she was doing for the company. He did this through his demeanor and lack of communication. It took her packing up her office and almost walking out because she was so irate with his attitude.

He would give her projects and then transfer them to someone else to complete. Someone who had more experience. Shaina confronted him and asked if she was capable enough to bring the project to a certain point of completion, why was she left out of the room, preventing her from understanding and learning the process? She let others know this was unacceptable. She argued this sentiment: "If you don't want to put me in the position to be working through the final decisions, let me sit in the room. How else am I ever going to learn if you are not teaching or training me, lifting me up to carry through?"

Shaina says this leader was "retirement age." He was working with the only female in the group, and somewhere he decided since she was half his age, she didn't know anything. Was he intimidated? Yes!

She told him that "eventually I am going to take your place." This leader retired a short time later, and as he was leaving told Shaina that he "respected her attention to detail and her strong work ethic." He told her she was going places.

The other challenge she faced, and one we have all

faced, is sitting across the table or in a room with a group of operators who wonder why you are there and if you understand the business.

Have you had any pivotal experiences while at TMS?

We talked about the bidding process and what the team expends in terms of time and energy to prepare the bids. They have worked nights until 8 or 9 p.m. for weeks on larger projects. They attack the project from every aspect. For example, how is the customer and our competitors viewing this project? Is there another aspect of the contract we should be looking at? All the complexities are brought into the equation. Even though this process is exhausting, the exercise is never quite the same because management, oper-ations, or business philosophies vary. In other words, you second-guess through the entire process. But she acknowledges that you learn something new every time you go through the exercise, about yourself, co-workers, and the capabilities of the company.

When you win you are on top of the world. She admits that it is the losses that often propel you to the win column. She says she beats herself up when they lose a contract and encourages everyone involved to examine what the team could have done differently.

"I don't really keep a notch on the belt for the wins. I take the stripe on my back for the losses."

What have you learned about yourself?

Shaina prides herself on being confident in knowing

what she is capable of. "That's just how women find their way in corporate America, in a man's world. Just anywhere. Whatever you do, don't dare let others make you feel like you're incapable of doing what they are capable of doing."

She has also learned that when she falls on her face, "it's hard, it sucks, but you pull the gravel out of your teeth and move one. You learn the most in those pain points, so I don't regret anything."

Shaina has learned that she is capable of more than she thought. If she doesn't constantly challenge herself and if others don't challenge her, she may just stagnate and not grow. She is amazed by the amount of growth she's experienced both personally and professionally over the last nine years at TMS. She attributes a good portion of that growth to mentors and supporters in the company encouraging her to accept new challenges.

Is there anything you would like to see changed in your company?

She would like to understand the succession planning process. She wonders why there is no apprenticeship program for bright, shining stars in the company. Programs could be designed to prepare star performers to fill senior and mid-management vacancies within the company as compared to someone coming in from the outside. Shaina does realize, however, that there may be extenuating circumstances for someone being recruited from outside the company.

She says, "If I were to ask what my succession plan is in the company ten years from now, I am not sure

I would get an answer, but I will tell them: My plan today for me within five years is to be VP of Marketing."

How did your company respond to the COVID-19 crisis?

She felt the company was extremely responsive and respectful of employees' personal situations in terms of children, school, extended family care situations, etc. She said the company is very family-oriented from top management down. Employees were provided with computers and whatever else they needed to be able to do their jobs from home. While Shaina traveled during this time, the silver lining for her was being able to spend more time with her four daughters and husband. Since extracurricular activities were canceled, they were all together. She says it has been an "upside-down experimentation in this world" and has loved having this time with her girls. She adds, "You take care of what is most important to you."

Have you resolved to accomplish anything or create anything at TMS?

Shaina is committed to being successful. She is also trying to encourage more women from the company to get involved in AWMI and help network both internally and externally.

Shaina is a big advocate of picking up the phone to have a conversation versus emailing and texting, which those in their twenties and thirties prefer. She is committed to "busting" them out of that habit and be more communicative.

She is also diligent about meeting with customers and getting to know them personally. Having that personalization with customers makes a big impact, and she has witnessed the older marketing individuals doing this for years. "It is their key ingredient for success."

Shaina says, "We have lives outside of our jobs," and when you take the time to personalize your relationships with people, you are going to be successful. When people feel valued, their performance is positively impacted, profitability is impacted, and the return is exponential. "When you put a smile on your face and care about people, that is all it takes."

What is unique about being a woman in the steel industry?

She feels she has a great opportunity because of the big push for diversification. "If I identify something I am interested in, and work towards it, it can happen and there is no reason why it couldn't. If I set myself up to believe that I have no opportunity, then I won't. If I don't take the steps to position myself, if I don't work and improve my abilities and build the relationships, then I won't go anywhere. I know what it will take, I know what I am capable of, and if you have the drive, you can be successful in the steel industry. You just keep working at it. I don't think there are any roadblocks for me today like there were thirty years ago."

She says she wants to understand what the women in the industry who came before her experienced. She had a small taste of that when she first joined the company. "It just made me grit my teeth, a little bit more, like *I'll show you*."

Do you see any disadvantages to being a woman in the steel industry?

Shaina feels that one of the disadvantages was being taken seriously by the old guard, part of the good ol' boys club. Fortunately, she sees this lessening with retirements and the integration of younger people. She says, "I don't like playing fear into a role of opportunity." That troubles her. "Accusation without merit is appalling. Women have a greater opportunity today."

Have you ever felt any pressure to cut corners from a safety standpoint?

We stand by some cardinal rules on safety and there is no tolerance whatsoever for cutting corners on safety.

How do you balance being female and being surrounded by a lot of men?

Shaina has four girls. When she comes home from work, she is immediately immersed in their lives and her husband's. She tells a recent story about her ten-year-old who went into her closet, put on a pair of her slacks, her blazer, and heels and then picked up the phone like she was having a work conversation, totally mocking Shaina. They all laughed.

She says she tries to have a "light heart" and be understanding about the differences between males and females. As a comparison, she mentions her husband is very vocal about the details of his day while Shaina says she doesn't bring her work life into the family environment and vice versa. Wherever she is is where her focus is 100 percent. She "finds the balance is just focusing on what you have to deal with right at hand and then move on."

I asked Shaina if she felt adequately compensated and how she would encourage women to have this discussion if they did not feel adequately compensated.

She feels adequately compensated now, but says she had to fight for it and take a stand when she had been with the company only a few years. It took more than one conversation and more than one request. She knew management understood that she could go elsewhere. She did her homework on what her value was and stuck to her guns.

When she approached management, she says she "had to think her way through it," but she always went back to the facts. She looked for two or three job postings that were close to what she was doing and looked at what the company was offering to pay a new hire. She calculated the number of years she had been with the company, including cost of living increases and bonuses, and determined what her value was.

As she says, "No one is going to set that value for you." The company "sets a value for a job, they set a value for the position, but if you have more qualifications, you have to highlight who you are, what you bring to the table, what your own goals and expectations are for yourself within the company." That is exactly how she laid it out to management. She told them she was committed to staying with the company, she was committed to being successful personally and see-ing the company continue to be successful. She told them they weren't going to find that level of dedication with "everybody that comes in and answers a job posting."

Do you see any barriers for women coming into the industry today?

Shaina feels that if a woman has a stellar resume, a track record of success, she would have an advantage today in getting hired at not only entry levels but at middle management and executive levels, because of that drive for diversification.

What skills do you think women add to the workplace environment?

Shaina says "women bring a different level of compromise" when it comes to evaluating situations, whether it is contract negotiations or sales. Women aren't afraid to suggest a new way of looking at a situation versus how it may have been done in the past. While she acknowledges you might get some pushback, she says "men like a challenge" and it might end up you are able to convince someone to do a trial. And if not, Shaina laughingly says, "they get the trophy, and I don't."

What is your reputation at the company?

About a year ago, an executive at the office passed Shaina in the hallway and asked how her projects were going. She told him she was dealing with one of their more difficult contracts, to which he replied, "You can handle it better than these boys because I heard you are quite the shark."

She says her reputation is that she is a fighter. "I am going to stand up for the company. I am going to stand up for what's right." Shaina is very "black and white. If this is the expectation and if it is off, then I am going to bring it back to balance. If you fight me on it, I am going to ask you why." Everyone feels like she is this tough person. Basically, she is known as a "ball buster." As laid-back as she says she is, "when it is time to focus on business, my expectations are great."

Have you experienced any on-site accidents or deaths?

Recently, an employee at one of their sites had a heart attack and died. He was still young. Management encouraged anyone who needed to take some time off to grieve to do so, and they were even prepared to shut down the mill if the crews needed that time.

Shaina commented that the people at the sites spend more time with co-workers than they do their own families. The feelings of brotherhood, sisterhood, and family are strong. Shaina says some of the guys call her "little sister," and she doesn't hesitate to refer to the guys as "her brothers." I heard this from a lot of people I interviewed.

Immediately after the death, three company vice presidents were onsite to evaluate any safety breaches. They also were in communication with the men and women on the shift, even following up with the crews to see if they needed any time off and to evaluate how they were dealing with the loss.

Shaina has been overwhelmed with the level of support and caring everyone shows co-workers following any family tragedy. The company also has funds they distribute to employees who are struggling financially due to various issues. Shaina had a medical scare and the company encouraged her to take whatever time she needed to address her situation. The company seems genuinely concerned for the welfare of their employees.

Does your job encroach on your personal life?

She says it is quite the opposite. The company fosters a family-oriented atmosphere. There has never been a situation where she felt she had to sacrifice family time for her company.

Have you ever been told anything that has motivated you professionally?

Shaina is grateful to her mentors for telling her that if she is ever put in a compromising position, she shouldn't for one minute think she has to "adhere" to anyone telling her she needs to do something that she feels is morally or ethically wrong, personally or professionally. While she feels fortunate that she has never been put in that position, she knows she has people to fall back on who will support her if she is "pushed into a corner."

She likes to quote Tom Hanks in the movie *A League of Their Own*. It was about the All-American Women's Baseball League that was started in this country during WWII when the men were over in Europe fighting. In one scene, Hanks scolds one of the women ballplayers on his team, who is crying: "Are you crying? There is no crying in baseball."

Don't sit there and become stagnant. Get up and keep going. If you failed, cool, we all do. Now figure a way out." She feels it's on you to make it work. She says there is always "room for growth. Just figure it out."

Shaina has everything she needs to continue to be successful in this industry or anywhere she would want to go. I think we are fortunate to have someone who sees value in this industry, in the products we supply, in the relationships that allow us to think of some co-workers as brothers and sisters and families. Where do you see that in the dot com and high-tech companies today?

Are there any generalities people make about the company or the industry that you would like to see changed?
Shaina says, "Why is a woman working in the steel industry? Let's change that."

* * *

We ended our interview by Shaina saying she doesn't see many women plant managers, but she says, "You can do it." She sees a trickle of women working their way up in the production side. "I would just like to see more diversification." She feels that if you could "open up a window into what this industry has to offer and what a staple it is in our everyday life," then more women might consider working in the industry. She uses herself as an example. She had no clue what the steel industry was all about, and she still thinks it is a secret out there in terms of the opportunities it can provide to not only women but men as well.

Shaina doesn't see barriers in this industry. As someone else mentioned that I interviewed, she only sees opportunities. She isn't afraid of hard work. She isn't afraid to speak up or fail. She believes in pushing forward, learning, and figuring it out. She has a five-year plan to become VP of Marketing, and I have no doubt she will. She embodies the power of passion, conviction, and strength. Go Shaina!

Thank you.

About TMS International

TMS International (formerly known as Tube City IMS) leads our industry with a comprehensive and pioneering array of pre- and post-production mill services for global steelmakers. We are experts in on-site services, including scrap purchasing and optimization, inventory management, logistics, metal recovery, slag processing, steel scarfing, surface conditioning, refractory removal, and maintenance.

We pride ourselves on delivering unrivaled service to our partners every day, on every contract, everywhere we operate around the world.

See why we have been the leading outsourcing partner in North America since 1926 and continue to grow throughout the world.

To learn more, visit TMSInternational.com

Chapter Nine

Catherine Walsh

Steel Trader

Stories from a Steel Trader—
"You have to know how to work the deal."

"I've always loved politics," Cathy Walsh says, "and as I look back on my career, I realize I was privileged to witness firsthand many world events. My father taught me at an early age that for a country to become a first-world country they needed a steel industry. He was right.

"My travels took me behind the Iron Curtain during the 1980s and 1990s. I traveled to East Germany, Hungary, Russia, Latvia, Estonia, Yugoslavia, and Romania. My steel trade deals were made with state agencies, steel mills, and trading companies. I was working in the international trade industry during the time of communism, glasnost, and then privatization. The stories and characters from that time are beyond belief. My travels also took me to Germany, Finland, Brazil, Argentina, Venezuela, Turkey, Egypt, and Mexico. I also lived in Canada for several years. It's been a great adventure meeting and experiencing so many cultures as I moved seamlessly from trading prime and secondary steel with domestic mills, foreign mills, trading companies to working with logistics companies, and banks."

Cathy is in her forty-sixth year in the steel industry. Her career path has been nontraditional. She is one of the few industry executives who can say they worked for a domestic mill, an international trading company, a service center, and is a business owner. For more than twenty years, she worked from her home as an independent contractor. Since January 2010, she has been working with Mill Steel in Grand Rapids, Michigan. Prior to that she was with Toyota Tsusho as a trader/contractor for eight years.

Due to her diverse background, Cathy has worn many hats and works best with those companies who understand a trader's mentality. She negotiates with steel mills both domestically and internationally and purchases both prime and secondary steel. "Every day is different and full of opportunity." This work ethic is why Cathy feels she operates best as an independent contractor. She is willing to work odd hours and take the risk in return for the higher reward. Financial independence has always been her single greatest motivator.

By the way, Cathy and I graduated from the same high school. She was on the World Affairs Council in high school and attended world affairs events in the Pittsburgh area. She was the oldest of five siblings, three girls and two boys. She reminded me that we were co-captains of the girls' volleyball team.

Cathy at 21

170

We also competed against one another in a summer swimming league. I was the sprinter, and she was stronger in the long distances.

Cathy grew up in Wexford, Pennsylvania. Her Italian mother and Irish father were first-generation Americans. Her mother's parents spoke only Italian. She credits her parents' immigrant background for the wisdom, influence, and advice they shared with her growing up and as an adult.

Cathy went to Penn State main campus as a freshman. They had only started admitting women to the main campus as freshmen a year or two before. She thinks she got to the main campus because of her swimming abilities. She played on the first women's water polo team, which she enjoyed.

She started as a physical education major but realized she wouldn't make any money with that major, so knowing her strengths and weaknesses she decided on economics. She thought this major would give her more opportunities and that economics wouldn't involve as much math, which she realized too late was an incorrect assumption. She minored in Russian because she was fascinated by Soviet politics and thought there might be some interesting opportunities for a career. She had attended Catholic school until ninth grade where the nuns had taught her about communism and the Cold War. Her interest and immersion into the Russian language and culture was a result of those experiences and her high school participation in the World Affairs Council.

Cathy's dad was vice president of finance for an engineering company in Pittsburgh. The company designed and built burners for the blast furnaces and the open-hearth furnaces. Since the HR department reported to her dad, he was involved in the USW contracts for the employees. She also had an uncle who worked at U.S. Steel. Her mom had her degree in English and was the first woman manager at Quaker State Oil.

Cathy was eager to finish college and start creating her path to financial independence. Her dad encouraged her to finish and graduate "so she could write her own ticket." After graduating in 1975, the Pittsburgh area was in a recession. Cathy was able to secure the name of a college recruiter at U.S. Steel and literally knocked on the door at 600 Grant Street and refused to leave until she could talk to someone. The effort worked and three days later she was offered a job at their plant in Worcester, MA.

U.S. Steel had an electrical wire and cable plant in Worcester, and they needed an inside salesperson. After a little more than a year, management decided to close the plant and Cathy was laid off. She packed up her belongings and moved back to Pittsburgh. She admits she learned a lot and that the experience was hard, not because she was a woman, but because she was twenty-two, she didn't know anyone, and living conditions were not favorable.

Cathy took six months to travel out west, came back to Pittsburgh, and called U.S. Steel. She wanted to know what they had available in Bucks County, Pennsylvania, outside of Philadelphia. It turned out they had a two-year management training program, comparable to Bethlehem's looper program, with an opportunity at the Fairless Hills facility, so Cathy packed her bags again and headed to Fairless.

While she was in the two-year program, Cathy figured out she could make additional money working swing shifts. She worked as a foreman for about six months in the pipe mill. During this time, she developed a great respect for the crane and shift operators. She said they worked hard and knew what they were doing. They would frequently work thirty-six-hour shifts and when she asked them why, they said, "You got to be somewhere." This approach to living life remains with her even today.

Her sister joined her in the pipe mill, and it was her sister's job to scrape the slag out of the reheat furnaces. One day she was watching her sister work and Cathy realized how dangerous this job was. She got her sister out of the mill.

Corporate eventually discovered Cathy was working the swing shifts. The general manager at the mill gave her an ultimatum: either work in the mill or stay in the sales training program. Cathy chose to continue in the sales program even though she knew she would make less money in the short term. After twelve months at the mill, she was assigned to inside sales in Philadelphia for a year. The training program continued in Pittsburgh for several weeks where all the trainees from around the country met for the first time. They traveled to several mills and were initiated into the big picture of U.S. Steel by all departments in the company. The legal department spent a few days instructing the trainees as to the legalities of doing business. It was this training that Cathy credits with learning to mitigate risk for herself and her employers.

U.S. Steel training also emphasized taking responsibility for your actions. An outside sales rep was expected to coordinate all activities between the company and the customers.

After a rigorous two-year program, Cathy was assigned to the New York sales office located in Saddlebrook,

New Jersey. She was the first outside woman in sales in the company.

With her business suit and bowtie blouse, she began calling on customers who were not shy about telling her, "We don't deal with women—give me a man." Other than one customer, she had good business relationships with most of them.

In 1983, she told her boss she was bored and asked what her next move would be. The traditional career path at U.S. Steel was a larger territory in another state, which would entail multiple moves. Cathy knew this was not the lifestyle she wanted to live.

One of her responsibilities in the NJ office was to call on Kurt Orban Company, Inc., which was the first steel importer in the country. In 1983, there was no internet or import data collection and the mills relied on their sales reps to call on the importers and try to elicit information for dumping suits. She wrote reports and got to know the players in the import market. One

The "secret to the steel trading business: Know an opportunity when it presents itself. Know how to make lemonade out of lemons" and finally; "buy low, sell high and get your money."

day there was a job opening in the Kurt Orban Company, Inc. and she was offered a position as flat rolled steel product manager. Orban doubled her salary, and Cathy bought her first house in New Jersey.

In late 1983, she started traveling internationally. Her first trip was to Venezuela. After that she traveled to Mexico and spent the next two years traveling behind the Iron Curtain, trading with the Romanians and East Germans. At that time, the communist governments controlled everything, and the sale of steel products was through state agencies. In the mid-1980s, communist Romania and East Germany had least-favored-nation status, which meant they were charged duties two and a half times higher than non-communist most-favored-nation countries. The communist countries needed hard currency for their countries to function and at that time steel was the currency. Prices were extremely low and there were no trade restrictions in the United States other than the harmonized tariff system. The importers purchased hundreds of thousands of tons of steel but focused primarily on hot rolled, cold rolled, galvanized, and plate on speculation from those countries. The importers and the international banks worked together in financing raw materials to keep the trading between nations alive. The banks were willing partners in financing such huge quantities without the risk management of today because they were greatly exposed and were looking for payment from their communist country debtors.

Imported steel was bought on speculation, meaning there were no specific orders for incoming steel from domestic users, although there were imports that were purchased to fill domestic orders, which is known as back-to-back.

On one side you had the steel importers bringing in steel without it being sold first to a domestic user. On the other side you had the various steel groups filing $1M trade cases against dumping.

Kurt Orban Company merged with a German trading company and became DB Orban Company in 1984. It was this merger that Cathy first became exposed to the high-flying German trading community. Cathy said she was a moth to the flame. These older and more experienced traders lived on the edge. As a young trader she learned the art of the deal and learned about the world, politics, and money.

Cathy was the only female international steel trader at DB Orban and in the country. She was also the only woman traveling overseas to negotiate contracts for imported steel to be shipped to the United States and Canada.

Cathy remembers sitting with representatives of the state-owned Hungarian steel mills. They were all women. The head deputy of the Hungarian steel industry looked at Cathy and said, "You're the pioneer. We have never seen a woman from the United States." There she was surrounded by women, controlling an industry dominated by men in most other countries. Cathy immediately bonded with the Hungarians, and they did a lot of business together.

She loved going to Turkey. It is a Muslim country and to her, Turkey was exotic and one of her favorite places. The traders she met in Turkey were always making the next deal, which she loved. It was here that she learned how interwoven the steel industry was. Every person at every step of the way expected a commission.

Cathy focused on purchasing carbon flat roll, but she also bought stainless bar and coils. These purchases would take her to Sweden and Finland. Stainless bar came from Finland. She learned to eat reindeer meat and drink vodka in those countries.

* * *

How did you get along with Kurt Orban?

"Kurt was probably in his late 60s when I joined his company and he was a gentleman." With his red pen he would critique or comment on every bit of correspondence that came in and left his office. Kurt was a pioneer and Cathy valued his guidance.

Within DB Orban Company was a group of older, well-established German traders who tried to make her life miserable. One of the traders competed with Cathy internally because they both bought and sold flat roll steel. She would go into his office, and he wouldn't even look up at her, and on more than one occasion told her to get out of his office. Cathy knew that she was a threat to him. Working with them made her realize that if you don't take risks in life you aren't going to get ahead. Cathy said these traders "risked it all every day." They were willing and able to step up and do enormous steel trades on speculation. They would open letters of credit to the mills without having sold one ton of steel. This is unheard of today.

Cathy states that this speculation eventually brought about drastic changes in the international trading business. During the late 1980s and mid-1990s there were millions of tons of steel brought into the US market unsold. This practice led to the downfall of many trading companies, and it damaged the domestic steel industry. Oversupply of steel caused the market to crash and domestic mills to go out of business and suffer great losses.

The times were changing, and Cathy found herself out of a job. In early 1986, she jumped from the international trading world to a domestic service center, Edgecomb Metals in Bensalem, Pennsylvania. She combined forces with a previous colleague who had been her sales rep for DB Orban in the Chicago area. He was already entrenched in the secondary steel world and the two went on to run a successful secondary steel division. During this time, Cathy purchased imported steel overseas and established additional lines of credit for the company.

While she was at Edgecomb, Cathy's colleague introduced her to yet another tier of steel movers and shakers, a.k.a. the entrepreneurs. The entrepreneurs were often second and third-generation family-owned businesses. They were colorful, but no-nonsense. Their risk management style went beyond a credit report. It was here she learned that character counts. In Cathy's experience, if a person or a company has a history of slow payments, claims, or bankruptcies, it is likely this pattern of bad business habits will repeat itself. Balance sheets can be manipulated but behavior seldom changes.

In 1987, Cathy married a fellow trader and moved their family to Montreal. Because Cathy was not completely fluent in French and did not have the proper visas to work in Canada as an employee, she began the first of her entrepreneurial endeavors. Cathy began working as a sales rep from her home in Montreal for a trading company in the United States. She also began buying and selling steel for her own account.

While in Montreal, she put together one of the largest deals of her life. Jamaica had been devastated by a hurricane, and building materials were needed to begin reconstructing houses and businesses. She bought and sold 30,000 tons of galvanized .013 roofing stock that would ship to Jamaica to be used for rebuilding. She ran this deal through a trading company and collected a commission. While still in Montreal she did a secondary deal that was shipping to Turkey. For this deal Cathy had received a letter of credit from the Turkish customer and had purchased the steel with her own funds. When her vessel arrived to load the cargo, Cathy went to the Port of Montreal to inspect the steel in the vessel and found it covered in pigeon dung. She had already purchased the steel and paid for the vessel. A clean bill of lading from the captain was the stipulation within the letter of credit. Without this clause the bank would not pay the vendor. Cathy's personal money was on the line. She found a broom, donned a hazmat suit, went down into the hold of the ship, and started cleaning off the coils. She received the clean bill of lading and a few days later she had her money from the bank.

Cathy also told me about a deal her husband had negotiated for pipe and wire rod. It turned out his vessel was hijacked coming out of Turkey. Lloyds of London, the cargo insurer, traced the steel to Libya. It had been stolen and sold to the Gaddafi regime. At the time there was a trade embargo and Libya needed the steel. The country's only option was to either steal it themselves or purchase the stolen cargo.

After her husband's contract ended in Montreal, they moved to Westport, Connecticut. Upon arriving in Westport with two small children, she teamed up with another friend who owned Mainline Metals and began buying and selling secondary steel from her home. Again, she was with a colorful entrepreneur who loved to teach common sense business basics via a series of one-liners such as, "Loose lips sink ships; Stop talking and listen; Dot, period, end of discussion; I'll never do business with him ever again—until the next time; Character counts; Do you know anyone who knows him?" Her favorite quote is: "Don't let a problem fester. Address it right away before it gets worse." This adage coupled with "Own up to your mistakes" continues to guide her life today.

Cathy says she had an opportunity to work with many legendary traders. They were all smart, all entrepreneurs, who made fortunes and they didn't care if Cathy was female or not. They loved her. She was cute, funny, and tough, and she continues to have a great sense of humor. She also enjoyed working with men. She knew what she was doing and was able to get into the mills to do it. The product was of no consequence; it was only about being able to make a profit. This she understood.

According to Cathy, knowing an opportunity when it presents itself is key to being a trader. Knowing how to make lemonade out of lemons is also key. She shared the following instances.

When one of the mills was commissioning a new hot roll mill around 1986, she and her colleague were approached about buying the startup tons from the commissioning. The team from Edgecomb flew to Alabama, where they selected and marked the 1,200 tons of secondary hot roll coils that were to be loaded into a barge and shipped to Chicago. Being too trusting, Cathy and her co-worker left the mill and the general manager decided to ship coils that were destined to be scrapped versus the coils they had earmarked for Chicago. When the coils arrived in Chicago it was quickly determined they had been taken advantage of. Fortunately, they had the foresight to hold up paying the invoice until the cargo was inspected in Chicago and the deal was salvaged. The mill settled the claim. They learned a lesson in human nature, but the previous year's training taught them how to handle the situation correctly. It is noteworthy that after this incident the general manager at the mill was fired.

During the same period a trading company sold Cathy 11,000 tons of cold rolled steel coils from Yugoslavia. The trader reneged on the deal, leaving Cathy and her company liable for the tons. Previous experience and lots of chutzpah enabled Cathy to figure a way to hold the trading company accountable for the anticipated losses. They filed a breach of contract suit against the trader and the trader was forced to pay.

In 1997 Cathy joined Seco Steel Trading as their vice president of sales. When the company was caught up in the Arcelor/Mittal merger, she moved on.

For the third time in her career Cathy teamed up with her good friend from Edgecomb who was now working with Toyota Tsusho America, Inc. In 2002, she became an independent contractor and returned to importing flat rolled steel. This time there was no speculation, and everything was presold. Cathy was her own profit center and responsible for every aspect of the business, including chartering of vessels, drawing up letters of credit, securing the offerings, and pre-selling. Toyota was risk-averse, which was the opposite of her prior trading experience. However, there was still room for error, and anything could go wrong. Before embarking on new business ventures the question asked was always, "Do we know them?" Again, character and history were just as important as a balance sheet.

Being in international trade was always risky in the late '80s and beyond. It was literally the Wild West. In Cathy's view, it was always challenging because of human nature, politics, and the market. Lawsuits were common, so she knew to always be prepared and keep meticulous records. She told the story of one multimillion-dollar deal that went wrong. After analyzing all possible outcomes, she immediately set out to organize three different counter-suits. She was an independent contractor and two of the parties involved were threatening to come after her personally. She decided to step into the fire and go on the offense because she knew she was prepared and they weren't. Multiple depositions and six years later, a settlement was reached.

In 2009, a casual conversation with a steel confidant led to a discussion with Mill Steel Company in Grand

Rapids, Michigan. The owner of the company at that time understood trading and knew Cathy's reputation. They decided to take a chance with each other to build a business selling secondary. He cared about the bottom line and never tried to micromanage her. Twelve years later and many different assignments, Cathy continues to enjoy her relationship with Mill Steel.

Cathy says for her it was always about creating the best life/work balance for herself and her family. Money was always her major motivator. She never felt disadvantaged being a woman in this industry. In fact, she felt it was an advantage. She was able to work from home while her children were growing up and feels she had the best of both worlds.

Although she didn't feel disadvantaged, she did start to feel some pressure about her age. She says it was initially shocking when someone brought up her age since she doesn't view herself as old. When anyone comments now about her age, she brushes them off with humor, and challenges them to a competition.

Did you ever have any issues with anyone you worked with?
"Most of the issues I've had have been issues that are normal business issues."

She did say she had a German trader assault her in a limousine in 1984. She successfully fended him off and he apologized, saying he assumed she was a hooker.

What have you learned about traveling internationally and doing business internationally?

Cathy says you need to respect the different cultures, try to understand them, and figure out how to make the differences work around your agenda and theirs. You should always try to be conversant on what's happening in their country. Showing a sincere interest is the easiest way to gain their respect.

What has been most gratifying for you?

She feels fortunate to have worked with so many different traders and entrepreneurs. The traders taught Cathy about the world and how steel plays a vital part of every nation and the world economy. She was fortunate to begin traveling extensively at the early age of twenty-nine. She enjoyed the entrepreneurs because they were gregarious but tough. They taught her about life, business, and how to communicate more directly. In retrospect, she realizes how progressive all her employers have been. There were some bumps in the road along the way, but it was new territory for the steel industry to have women in management positions.

She remembers her high school teacher who put her on the World Affairs Council. Looking back over her life she sees certain themes that have been consistent over the years such as politics and the interplay between cultures.

She has been elected to public office in her hometown of Westport, Connecticut, multiple times. Public service gives her the personal satisfaction of being able to see the results of her efforts. She sees how her decisions on the planning and zoning commission for over thirteen years steered the growth of her town in the right direction. She is proud to have created parks, protected waterways, and facilitated major rehabilitations of many facilities in her town.

For her, trading steel is an adventure and a means to a lifestyle. Cathy has always placed a high priority on income, and that has been her focus in the steel industry. "If the doors are shutting in my face, then I zigzag and knock on another door, and I think that's the important thing: If it's closed, move on.

"I'm grateful to U.S. Steel and all my other employers who took a chance with me. I'm grateful for the long-lasting and deep friendships I have within the industry."

What have you learned about yourself?

She says she is very resilient, but she has also "learned to let go of stuff, to let go of things."

She admits that she is still focused on income, "just to build my war chest, stay relevant, and stay with my friends." She wants to make deals for as long as she can. Her goal is to be able to say she has been trading steel for fifty years. She is four years away from that goal.

Cathy looks back now and can see that it was her father's frequent business discussions that empowered her as a girl. They discussed politics, the world, wars, the Supreme Court, civil rights, risk-taking, and not living in fear. He encouraged her to go for it. She also feels she has learned from everyone she has met along the way.

Do you think women and men approach their jobs differently?

Cathy thinks women are more to the point and prefer to get the job done without a lot of fanfare. She feels one of the mistakes she made was she "never beat my own drum hard enough, and I think most women don't."

Did you ever feel discriminated against in terms of compensation?

"No, but I found I was underpaid in the beginning," Cathy says. "You have to ask for your money or you're not going to get it. I think that is the key. If you ask and don't receive it, move on and find another job."

She has been compensated with combinations of salary, bonuses, and commissions. "My income is really up to my ability to make profits.

"You have to rely on yourself to make things happen for you. You can't rely on anyone else. You are responsible for your own success."

What is your reputation in the industry?

"When the men in the male-dominated industry learned that I was serious and just wanted to make money, they let me into their inner sanctum. They trusted me and knew that I was focused and understood the business and would do it correctly and ethically. Today, I'm recognized as being someone who has been able to carve their own path in the industry and done it well. My career has been unconventional, but I continue to bring value to my principles. I'm recognized as being one of the first women outside sales reps in the country, the first woman international trader and a business owner."

I mentioned that trading had a reputation for being cutthroat and Cathy says that life can be cutthroat. She feels the trading world is more ethical than in the past. "it's squeaky-clean right now." Someone who has since retired told Cathy, "It's not how it used to be. I loved it when there was larceny in everybody's heart."

Cathy says "People recognize that I'm a workaholic and am successful." They do business with her because she has a good track record. She has only prepared one resume in her life and that was when she applied to U.S. Steel in 1976. Cathy credits her long relationships with her business colleagues with being the key to her success.

How can the industry attract more women?

"The steel industry offers endless opportunities for women: sales, manufacturing, accounting, finance, law, logistics, planning, IT, and the list goes on. The industry is highly involved in sustainability and is very much focused on the future. There are many women in the industry today, and steel companies continue to value and promote women to the highest levels.

What I also like about our industry is that it's a small world that is highly connected. It's a stable, progressive business and pays well."

* * *

As we concluded the interview, she says, "My world is my steel buddies, my steel industry. They are my family and have been for years and years. The steel industry is my life." And then she added, "Here's the secret to the steel trading business: Buy low, sell high, and get your money."
Spoken like a true steel trader.
Thank you, Cathy.

CHAPTER TEN

Kelly Dallas

Cleveland-Cliffs Inc.
Director of Engineering-Flat Rolled

"I don't have a problem stepping up if I need to and I don't have a problem stepping back if I need to."

K elly started out as a nontraditional student. Her husband was in the military, and they married right out of high school. Fast-forward ten years. After working at a lot of different jobs, Kelly wanted a more focused professional direction and decided to go back to school. She was good at math and science and selected mechanical engineering, even though she admits she didn't know exactly what an engineer did.

There were several options in northwest Indiana. She enrolled at what is now Purdue Northwest but was previously known as Purdue Calumet. Kelly had three children at the time. She needed to schedule her classes around their activities and school, but she worked hard and received her degree in mechanical engineering.

"It is important to have a champion within the company."

By her junior year, Kelly worked as an intern at U.S. Steel. The internship was ongoing and not your traditional summer internship, so Kelly was able to work full-time in the summers and part-time during the academic year. One of her professors had a working knowledge of the steel industry and told her about a scholarship opportunity through the Iron & Steel Society (ISS), one of the predecessor associations of AIST.

Upon graduation, she learned about an opportunity in the engineering department at Bethlehem Steel in Burns Harbor, Indiana, and accepted the position. She has been with the company for over twenty years. During those twenty-some years, the company changed ownership five times and is now owned by Cleveland-Cliffs.

Can you share with me some of your experiences in your career?
Kelly happened to be reflecting on her life and where she was in her pre-teen years, which is the age of her granddaughter. She was thinking about some of the older TV reruns where the girls always chose to play dumb, so the boys would like them. She never identified with that image. Kelly always wanted to be the smartest person in the room and outshine everyone. She never felt she had to dumb herself down to get attention. She felt she started to shine in high school and noticed as she took more advanced classes there were fewer girls in the classes. In her pre-algebra class, there were only two female students.

Her father had a big influence on Kelly. She remembers a conversation with her dad, and they were discussing traditional female and male roles. Jokingly, he asked, "Why would you want to be a nurse if you could be a doctor?" In engineering, she has always been in the minority as there were more male students than female students, and that trend continues in the steel industry today.

She was always aware of the gender disparity, but because she was older than her teammates, she never felt any pressure because she was a woman. In addition, she had three children at home and didn't have time for issues or drama. She still finds herself in meetings where she is the only woman, but as she says, "I am usually the one running the meeting."

She notices that the camaraderie you have with male colleagues and co-workers is different. You may get along and they may be very respectful but there is still a difference. She may be invited to play golf, but it is not a casual invitation. There aren't any impromptu invitations to join a co-worker for lunch or dinner, or to go see a game. Kelly feels that one result of the "Me Too" movement is that men are even more reticent to invite women to join in activities either during the day or after work. She doesn't feel there should be any differences but there are.

She maintains that you need to find a balance. She admits to having thick skin from some of the slights that have been directed at her. The most recent incident occurred just after she was promoted to director of engineering. She was out to lunch with several colleagues (she hadn't been out to lunch since COVID-19). One of her colleagues asked what she was going to do next since she was finishing a big project. Kelly answered that her promotion meant that she was in fact now overseeing capital projects over various facilities. The conversation continued, and her colleague asked if she was reporting to a specific individual. "Actually, he reports to me now," she said. Their facial expressions registered pure shock. While her colleagues quickly regained their composure and complimented her, "their immediate reaction was not lost on me."

A few days later she was taking someone who reported to her around one of the offices because he was now in a management position and had never visited the facility. He asked Kelly if she would walk him through the facility and introduce him. As she was introducing him, a salesman in one of the offices immediately stood up and handed the new manager his business card and didn't even acknowledge Kelly. He didn't say "hi" or even make eye contact.

As we discussed the differences between men and women in the workplace, Kelly wondered if this salesman's behavior was purposeful or if his actions came from a bias he had with women working in the mills, or in the industry in general. Or perhaps he was simply dismissive, mistakenly thinking that she was an administrative person.

Kelly feels everyone has biases. Biases come from how you've been raised, outside influences, and your experiences, but that doesn't mean people can't learn and change the way they view things. We both agreed that the younger generations have grown up playing sports together, have been grouped together on academic teams or clubs, and have lived in coed dorms and on coed floors, so they don't see any differences. They don't care how they talk or who they are talking with, which is a positive step forward.

Kelly is seeing more and more women coming into production, as pipefitters, millwrights, etc. The numbers aren't large—one or two women here or there—but even though the work is hard, she believes these non-traditional positions offer great opportunities.

When someone does acknowledge you, Kelly says, it puts you in the spotlight, and not always in a good way. She remembered early in her career being in a big planning meeting for an upcoming mill outage. A lot of upper management were in the meeting. Kelly was the only woman in the room and was startled and embarrassed when her boss stood up in front of the room and asked her to take notes. She didn't mind taking notes because at that time it was not outside of her responsibilities, but she did mind being singled out in front of the group to do it. She would have preferred that her boss ask her prior to the meeting.

Another example of women being treated differently is when co-workers and subordinates apologize for using bad language. She feels that people need to say what they have to say however they say it. She prefers unfiltered speech to an amended communication style in the name of politeness.

Kelly has observed a lot of women who start to work at the company tend to leave. She doesn't know why and questions whether the overpowering male-dominated atmosphere or not knowing how to navigate the environment is a factor, or if women leave to have a family or move into more traditional careers. She wonders if the seasoned employees make the work environment difficult for these women in the plants and mills.

She feels it is important for women to see other women in positions of authority and executive management, whether it is an engineer, an astronaut, a vice president of production, part of a C-level team, or a CEO.

While she feels it will be a huge loss of tribal knowledge when baby boomers retire, she feels the bigger impact will be seeing more women promoted and advancing to higher positions in the company. She feels this visual will have a positive influence not only short-term but long-term.

When I interviewed Kelly, she was just finishing a four-year, $150M project at Burns Harbor. Commissioning was scheduled the week following our interview. In her new position she will manage the capital plans for nine facilities. Each mill has an engineering manager who oversees the details of the projects, and their respective regional managers report to her. She reports to the senior director of engineering.

Prior to Kelly's promotion, she was managing the financial budgets for the capital projects, so her job was more administrative in scope. She will now be managing people in this directorship position. There are three women engineers that work in her group.

WOMEN IN STEEL, WOMEN OF STEEL

Since the Cleveland-Cliffs acquisition of the Arcelor-Mittal USA facilities is fairly recent, management is still figuring out how everything is going to come together, but she is encouraged with management's commitment to quality projects and reliability, treating contractors fairly, and creating a more collaborative work environment between management and employees.

What is your definition of success?

She says very simply, "If you're happy most days in your personal and professional life you're doing a good job. If you're not happy most days, go do something else or get over yourself and figure it out."

What is your definition of failure?

She admits she is not a material person so material things are not important to her. She says you need to have pride in what you are doing, and if you aren't doing your best then you are failing. She advises you to ask yourself what is preventing you from doing your best.

What is your definition of happiness?

She defines happiness as accomplishing goals whether they are big goals or small goals.

What is the difference between a manager and a leader?

Kelly thinks a leader is someone you look up to and respect, someone you want to emulate. You can work for a manager who yells, screams, and gets things accomplished, but no one will respect them. Certainly no one looks up to them or chooses to lead like they do. "It's not about putting someone up on a pedestal; it's more about watching what they do and how they do it and thinking, *I can respect what they're doing.*" Finally, Kelly says, "Don't promote the yellers and the screamers." Instead, look at the people who are respected and getting the job done, running departments, and creating teams that people are proud to be a part of.

How do we develop more leaders in this business?

Kelly felt in the past, to be promoted, you had to have "the asshole gene." She gave me an example of this. Early in her career, two senior executives of the company came into a meeting she attended. You couldn't sit in certain chairs in the conference room because that was where they sat. They came in and sat down, didn't say hello or good morning or ask how the group was doing. The group was presenting a proposal for a big project and the executives were less than interested in the discussion. After the presentation, the executives left the meeting without a positive comment.

Look at the impact these executives had on a young professional woman. Many years later, this is what Kelly remembers about these two senior executives. Titles, yes. Leaders, no.

What Kelly is trying to do now is help those around her understand how important it is to have the right people in the right positions. The question she is asking everyone to consider when they are making decisions to hire and promote people is: "How will they fit and are they part of the team?" In other words, what is the culture of the company, of the department? How do we create a culture and what do we want that culture to look like? Finally, you need to make sure you hire the right people for the culture you are trying to build and support.

Kelly mentioned a recent situation in relation to this discussion about managers, leaders, and culture. On a particular project, although team members were committed to hitting a deadline, they wanted to let management know there was a potential problem with meeting the target dates. Rather than offering support or advise on how to mitigate the situation, the manager blasted out a derogatory email to everyone.

So, let's step back. Was it a CYA email, to make sure the problem and/or potentially missing the deadline wouldn't fall on his shoulders? Who was the "yelling and screaming" really for? It certainly wasn't meant to encourage the team; in fact, it alienated the team members. Title, yes. Leader, no.

What do you think women add to the workplace?

Kelly feels women bring a different perspective. When she was younger, she had little backup or support with her kids other than her husband. She couldn't afford to be at the office until seven or eight o'clock at night; she had to pick her kids up from daycare (when they were young) or be there for their extracurricular activities. It didn't mean she wasn't committed or dedicated to her job; she just had other responsibilities. She did what she needed to do and allocated her time appropriately. She needed flexibility to be able to be with her kids if they had a ballgame, event, etc. If you have never had to think that way or work that way, it is a stretch for some managers and co-workers to understand.

Kelly feels that all these different experiences, different voices, different expectations are part of the diversity that we need to understand in today's working environment. Women bring these conversations and priorities to the discussion table. Once her children were grown, this allowed Kelly to travel or work late as needed. But she still remembers when she didn't have that flexibility and how responsibilities at home impacted her at work. She says it is important to know your team, what their jobs are, what they can do, and where they feel challenged. But if you need time during the week to be flexible and can still get your job done then she supports that.

What are your thoughts about mentoring?

As part of a formal training/mentoring program, when she first started with Bethlehem, Kelly was assigned an engineer to not only train her, but he also became a mentor and is still a mentor to this day.

She also talked about the importance of having a champion. This is a theme that came up numerous times in my interviews. A champion is someone who acts as an advocate for you. It is someone who makes sure your name is mentioned when unique opportunities arise and where they think you would have the potential to excel. You may or may not know who they are or even what they are doing for you behind the scenes, but they are there nonetheless, making sure your name is in the hat when these opportunities present themselves.

What have been some of your biggest challenges?

Her biggest challenge was balancing raising her children, going to school full-time, having a husband who worked sixty hours a week in the restaurant industry, and working part-time herself. She remembers making dinner for her children, putting them to bed, and then doing her homework. She says, "You make time for what you have to do."

A colleague of Kelly's has a sign that says, "We do not live in a perfect land." She added "you just have to go do it." It won't necessarily be perfect.

Kelly grew up with the mentality that "women had to do it all—bring home the bacon, fry it up in the pan, and do whatever for your man." That was what the media was promoting at the time. Women felt they had to do it all. She realized, "If I am working full-time, I am not going to be the 'perfect' mom. There is compromise everywhere and you can't do it all by yourself. You have to figure out that balance and understand that for yourself."

She mentioned again that her children were "latch-key kids." "We had to do what we had to do because we didn't have outside support of somebody being there or grandma picking them up." Other than one semester when she had evening classes, she scheduled her classes during the day when her children were in school. "It was a plan. I had to plan it out—I had to figure it out."

How would people describe you?

She says she hopes people would say she "knows what she is doing. I am not overly ambitious. I don't have big aspirations to do things. I hold my own. I can relate to people. I am fair. When I introduce people, I say I work with these people. I don't say they work for me."

How do you balance being around men all the time? What do you do for yourself?

Kelly says, "I used to wear nice clothes when I was in the office." Because she has been involved in this big capital project for the last three years, "I've been out in a trailer working so I wear hoodies, jeans, and T-shirts." Now since she is going to be working in an office again, she is rethinking her wardrobe.

✽ ✽ ✽

As Kelly says, "I don't have a problem stepping up when I need to, and I don't have a problem stepping back when I need to. I think this is exactly where the leadership of this industry needs to go." Yelling and screaming are no longer acceptable ways to manage. As much as production numbers are important, so is retention. If someone is meeting production goals at the expense of employees, should they be rewarded when there is a shortage of experienced and motivated people to fill those jobs?

As we wound down our conversation, I asked Kelly how we could attract more women to the industry. She feels we need more venues where we can talk to women and let them know what opportunities are available within the industry. Women are encouraged when they see other women at conferences and conventions, seated at head tables, respected as subject matter experts, speaking, and leading as managers, as CEOs, as engineers, on production floors, and in pulpits.

Kelly has stepped up in her life and she has encouraged her teams to step up too, as individuals, as managers, and as leaders. Her career has been focused on working with her teams to create opportunities, solve problems, initiate incentives for capital improvements, educate and create awareness, and excel. I will look forward to seeing where Kelly chooses to excel next.

Thank you, Kelly.

About Cleveland-Cliffs Inc.

Cleveland-Cliffs is the largest flat-rolled steel producer in North America. Founded in 1847 as a mine operator, Cliffs also is the largest manufacturer of iron ore pellets in North America. The company is vertically integrated from mined raw materials, direct reduced iron, and ferrous scrap to primary steelmaking and downstream finishing, stamping, tooling, and tubing. We are the largest supplier of steel to the automotive industry in North America and serve a diverse range of other markets due to our comprehensive offering of flat-rolled steel products. Headquartered in Cleveland, Ohio, Cleveland-Cliffs employs approximately 26,000 people across its operations in the United States and Canada.

To learn more, visit clevelandcliffs.com.

CHAPTER ELEVEN

Jennifer Wylie Faines

PR *Digital Communications*
CEO

"Stand By Your Can"and "Captain Steel"

J ennifer's father and mother were artists. Her father was a commercial artist and the creative director for an advertising company. His clients were U.S. Steel and Rockwell International. "Dad was an illustrator, an incredible painter, and a gifted visual artist." She was fascinated with many of his projects and all of the "really cool stuff" he created.

Her mother was going to night school at Carnegie Tech, what is now Carnegie Mellon University, majoring in fine art. During the day she worked as a secretary at an advertising agency, where she met Jennifer's father.

Jennifer's mom was the daughter of first-genera- tion Lithuanian immigrants who settled in Duquesne in Pittsburgh. Her grandfather

Class of '82

worked at Duquesne Works, which is owned by U.S. Steel. Her mom and dad had three girls and Jennifer remembers her father would bring home paper samples that vendors would bring to him. There would be pens and magic markers. She and her sisters would spend hours in the basement coloring and cutting up paper samples.

The girls created their own magazines from start to finish. They made up stories and wrote their own articles. They cut out pictures from other magazines and inserted the pictures in their articles interspersed through the magazine. One time they created a fictional yearbook with fifty senior graduates. They drew pictures of each of the graduates and wrote mini bios below their picture. Each of the girls had their preferences; some of them chose to draw while others chose to write. Jennifer was the writer. She says this was how they entertained themselves on rainy days.

Jennifer wasn't afraid to try sculpting, ceramics, painting, anything that was creative, but something always kept pulling her in the direction of writing. Her father joked that she might want to reconsider going into PR or advertising because she wouldn't make any money. She didn't listen to him. She told herself, "I like to talk, I like to write, and I like to do creative things."

Jennifer went to Clarion University in Clarion, Pennsylvania, and received her BS degree in communications. In one of her advanced classes, she wrote a paper about a fictional character, who was really meant to be her in five to ten years. "My fictional character was working as a successful corporate executive in communications." Jennifer "knew what I wanted to do but wasn't sure how to get there."

When she was in college, she thought she should

probably move to New York City since that was where all the high-powered PR people were located. Jennifer thought she would go to work for "some fabulous major company."

Sometimes, though, "life has a way of giving you different options." Her mother was diagnosed with ovarian cancer and Jennifer wanted to be with her

Carol and her mother.

during her final days. She made the decision to stay in Pittsburgh and has never regretted that decision.

Jennifer says, "You never know where that inspiration for your next career move might come from." She was looking for a job the summer after graduation and happened to read an article in *Cosmopolitan* magazine about the first female bank president in the United States. The bank was Equibank, the third largest bank in Pittsburgh at the time. Jennifer realized that the bank must have a marketing or PR department, so she wrote to the president and told her how impressed she was with the article featuring her story in *Cosmopolitan*. The president of the bank wrote back to her on her embossed letterhead and thanked her for her letter. She told her she had forwarded her letter and resume to the senior vice president of HR, who also responded to Jennifer's letter and resume. The bank didn't have any openings at that time but said they would keep her letter on file.

Two and a half months later, the bank called Jennifer and told her they had an opening for a marketing communications coordinator and invited her to come to the bank for an interview. She got the job although she never thought her first job would be in banking. Jennifer loved the job. "It was exactly the right thing for me to get my career off the ground." In looking back at this experience, Jennifer says she never considered that it might be improper to just write to the president of the bank, but she adds, "It never occurred to me not to try."

Jennifer realized that if she wanted to move forward in her marketing communications career and public relations, she needed to work at Ketchum, Inc., which was the largest PR and advertising firm in Pittsburgh. If you could get a job at Ketchum, you could get a job anywhere. Two years after she left Equibank and went to work for Dollar Bank, she received a job offer from Ketchum. She stayed at Ketchum nine years.

At Ketchum she was in the PR department, but also worked with the advertising team for some clients. In PR, she worked on brochures, media relations, press briefings, special events, and trade shows.

One of her first assignments was with the American Iron and Steel Institute. AISI is a trade association for North American steelmakers, which dates to 1855. She didn't know anything about the organization, but she was always willing to try something new, so she said yes. Jennifer says, "She had a lot to learn about the steel industry and communications."

I asked her what the atmosphere was like at Ketchum. She says she was surrounded by an "incredibly talented group of people" whom she knew would support her efforts to work with AISI, but at the same time it was very competitive. Even in that environment, she was promoted three times during her nine years with Ketchum.

It was the 1990s, which was a tough business climate

for the steel industry. AISI was recognizing that competing industry trade associations were more aggressive about promoting their agendas. The steel industry needed to promote its importance to the domestic economy. In other words, the value of steel was a well-kept secret that needed more public exposure and more public awareness.

Jennifer's first committee assignment from AISI was with the Tin Plate Producers—the steel used for canned food. At that time aluminum cans were flooding the American market. The steel industry wanted to educate consumers on the benefits of using cans made from tin plate. Up until the introduction of aluminum cans, all canned goods were made from tin plate. At that time plastic food containers were just being introduced to the market. It was all the steel industry could do to compete not only with aluminum but plastic as well. This was a real PR and advertising challenge even though cans were 100 percent recyclable and made from recycled scrap. Unfortunately, the industry was transitioning away from BPA-lined cans, another huge marketing challenge. Steel cans just weren't sexy or perceived as safe.

Jennifer remembers her first PR brochure for AISI was the "life cycle of a steel can from cradle to grave."

Jennifer targeted the food producers through the National Food Processors Association and the Food Marketing Institute since they were the groups deciding which food packaging materials to buy.

At the trades shows the Ketchum team and Jennifer orchestrated AISI's booth as a full-scale take-off on the old TV show *American Bandstand*, with live music every fifteen minutes. Performers changed the song lyrics to deliver pro-canned food messages. For example,

Tammy Wynette's song "Stand by Your Man" became "Stand by Your Can."

They also created "Captain Steel." He was an actor who performed a *Star Trek* routine promoting steel cans, which was also a successful effort to create brand awareness.

Jennifer says the parody "was one way to start getting people to pay attention to continuing to use steel cans for food." The campaign also pushed hard to promote the fact that steel cans are 100 percent recyclable.

At the time of these PR campaigns, AISI created a new organization within AISI dedicated to steel recycling, which became the Steel Recycling Institute and a Ketchum client.

The PR campaign focused on the environmental and municipal organizations that were working on recycling programs. Ketchum wanted to create a partnership with these groups to promote municipal recycling solutions. So, Ketchum launched the Steel Recycling Partnership in ten major cities and sponsored events within these communities to "elevate the awareness for the inherent recyclability of steel." These campaigns encouraged municipalities to include steel cans among items accepted in city recycling bins and recycling in the municipality. As a result of these campaigns more and more municipalities began accepting steel. Again, another successful campaign

"It never occurred to me not to try."

with measurable results. The Steel Recycling Partner-ship campaign went on to win a Silver Anvil Award from the Public Relations Society of America, which is the equivalent of an Oscar in the public relations world.

Jennifer and Ketchum participated in another PR campaign in Washington, D.C., for Earth Day, to pro-mote recycling. Captain Steel was there and so was United States Senator John Heinz from Pennsylvania, not long before the popular senator was tragically killed in a plane crash. Senator Heinz shook Captain Steel's hand and an Associated Press photographer captured the handshake. The photo was in newspapers around the country, which helped elevate the recycling campaign. "They were telling a story that hadn't been told before," Jennifer said.

The publicity helped create a new audience that "might never have associated the industry with doing anything environmentally responsible."

Jennifer also began to work with the Automotive Applications Committee, another AISI committee in Detroit, Michigan. This was when the automotive industry began testing the use of aluminum panels for cars to meet federal mandates designed to increase fuel economy, lower fuel mileage, and decrease the weight of cars and trucks. To combat the incursion of aluminum, the steel industry began to develop high-strength steels. However, this created some PR chal-lenges because although the weight of the car could be reduced there were no guarantees this innovation would improve safety.

Sometime in 1993 Jennifer was speaking with one of her clients. He said that he didn't think the Internet was going away and asked her to learn everything she could about the World Wide Web and how someone creates a presence on the web. She was excited to get the Automotive Applications Committee of the AISI up and running with a website. This was one of the first websites Ketchum ever worked on.

Around the late 1990s Jennifer left Ketchum to work for one of her clients and become director of marketing for Pittsburgh.com. Her client at Ketchum was Cox Interactive Media, and Pittsburgh.com was part of a network of online city sites across the country. Cox tied the local websites to the company's traditional media properties. For example, Pittsburgh.com was the city site launched in partnership with WPXI-TV for Pittsburgh. Today it is now a part of WPXI-TV.

Her early adoption of a new form of media allowed Jennifer to get in on the ground floor of using technology and creating online communications. Cox was building city sites and online communities long before social media was even a thing.

After Pittsburgh.com, she moved on to become the director of public relations for a small advertising and communications firm in Pittsburgh for several years.

By this time Jennifer had been gone from Ketchum for a decade. One day Ketchum called her. They were still working with the Canned Food Alliance through AISI, and they needed someone to run PR for the Alliance. Her former employer made her an offer she couldn't refuse.

It was 2008 and in addition to working with the Canned Food Alliance, Jennifer began to work with other food companies such as Kellogg's cereal and breakfast foods like Pop Tarts and Frosted Mini-Wheats.

By this time Ketchum had become a public company and Jennifer found herself with more administrative tasks and less responsibility for actual accounts, a role she preferred. She stayed with the agency for two years and then decided it was time to start her own company. She was hesitant and uncertain, but Jennifer realized that over the years she had made a lot of contacts. She went back to the owner of the agency where she'd worked before and asked him if he would hire her as an independent public relations practitioner. He agreed and she knew she would have some clients to start. She negotiated office space for discounted rates at his company and she now had an address.

What were some of your challenges over your career?

Jennifer says something I have heard frequently in my interviews and that is the feeling of "not being enough," what she describes as the imposter syndrome and that fear of "being found out." Something a lot of us have experienced in our careers.

One of quotes that ran through Jennifer's mind was, "Fake it till you make it. That means being confident in your abilities, even if you're scared. Eventually the confidence becomes genuine."

Jennifer had many opportunities to launch a big PR communications firm but didn't want the administrative headaches of managing overhead and staffing.

What has been most gratifying?

Jennifer sincerely enjoys helping people tell their story and "connecting the dots"—creating connections between clients' markets or products, and their customers' needs and interests.

One of her clients told her, "I love working with you, because I can just dump out a whole bunch of random thoughts and you string them together and make the most beautiful pearl necklace out of it. You string all these little pearls of wisdom together in just the right way."

What are you most proud of?

She is most proud of "doing what I love on my terms." She is proud she made the decision to create her own company and go her own way.

What is your idea of success?

"When it comes to career success," she says it is, "When you are in that spot where you're making positive material contributions by doing what you love and in the way you love doing it." Jennifer admits she could have made a lot more money if she had wanted to, but realized she is happy and content with her decision to have her own firm. "There are compromises everywhere."

She says, "The best successes are incremental successes because we are all works in progress and because life is a journey. You might have some setbacks along the way to becoming successful, but again, it is not about the destination; it is all about the journey."

"Success is constantly being redefined for me, and the moment I stop being curious and inquisitive is the moment I stop being successful."

What is your definition of failure?

"Not trying, at least to make the effort." She adds, "Failing is being too afraid to try. It is scary to get out there and go out on a limb and try, but what are the alternatives? Do nothing?"

What is your definition of happiness?

"I am an eternal optimist, and the glass is always half full. Happiness is a choice." She says she could have chosen to be unhappy. She lost her mother, father, and two sisters to cancer. But "I choose to appreciate the quality time I had with every member of my family. It's not quantity; it's about quality. And even though my time with them wasn't long, it was wonderful."

Jennifer also says, "When you make peace with yourself, the world around you seems to be a lot more peaceful." She feels "extraordinary happiness just being content and finding inner peace.

"Who you are right here, right now, at this moment in time, and appreciating exactly where you are, brings happiness."

What do you bring to the table that is unique?

She remembers at Ketchum when she was first hired. There were six account executives, and they would wonder which of the six would be promoted to senior account executive. The group relied on and expected Jennifer to ask the tough questions at management meetings because they were afraid to. It never occurred to Jennifer to be afraid to speak up.

Jennifer remembers when she was just starting out and was late for a meeting. There were fifteen men in the room and her. When she apologized for being delayed, they said, "We think we can overlook it since we all get to look at your legs now." Jennifer says she was mortified inside, but didn't miss a beat. "Well, that's very nice of you to notice, but that's not why we're here today, so why don't we just get started." It never occurred to her *not* to make a comment.

When Jennifer was a child, her parents encouraged her to speak up. She says her parents encouraged all three girls to do whatever they loved to do. Her mom taught her to face her fears and not be afraid to try anything new or say what's on her mind.

She says she had to compete with her two sisters. Her oldest sister, who was quite brilliant but rebellious, tested out of two different languages before she entered high school. She taught herself how to speak French and German. Her mother called her other sister "good-time Charlie." She was very smart too and yet didn't identify with the intellects at school. She became a party girl and had lots of friends. Jennifer felt she had the best of both worlds from two very different yet extremely talented sisters.

Where can you go with a communications degree?
Jennifer says she gets this question all the time and it is why she is frequently asked to speak at colleges and universities. She explains that someone who is creative, who is a good communicator/speaker, and/or likes to write should look at marketing communications as

a career. PR is a part of that broad category and can include employee communications, crisis communications, media and labor relations, event planning, product launches, video production, technical writing, and social media. The bottom line: "Every industry needs to communicate."

She says know yourself well enough to find out what skills you like to use and want to develop, and what skills aren't quite so strong. You may also discover along the way a skill set that you had no idea you possessed. "The rest often comes along just by being open to possibilities."

In this field you need to be a quick study. You need to know how to ask the right questions and know the correct person to ask. "You don't have to have all the answers, but you need to know which questions to ask."

Sometimes, she says, the information you need to present is very technical, so you need to be able to take the information and translate it into a way that people can understand and act upon. She says one of her projects was creating a crisis communications plan for manufacturing plant managers. The COVID-19 pandemic presented a new set of communications challenges. Executives were forced to communicate with employees during this time about new health and safety issues, social distancing, and working from home, as well as communicating with suppliers, customers, local communities, politicians, and shareholders. Working with companies that have facilities in multiple countries meant communicating through different national COVID-19 responses and restrictions, and cultural and language barriers. A major challenge early in the pandemic was to communicate the necessity that refractory businesses supporting the steel industry needed to stay open during COVID-19 because they were essential. This was strategic and crisis communications at its best.

You can see how many options someone with the skill sets discussed above would have in the steel industry, manufacturing, or steel-related associations.

What have you learned about yourself?
"The only thing that ever holds me back is myself."

* * *

Jennifer says she rarely has regrets, "because whatever decision I made at the time was the best decision I could have made at the time," given the information she had.

She would have loved to have had children. She thought she had plenty of time and everyone told her, "You can have it all. You can be a corporate executive and have children somewhere along the line...and then I woke up one day and I was older; I didn't have time.

"I've learned my life is much better when I try to stay present and stay in the moment, even while having aspirations and goals. I learn from the past and *plan for* the future, but I can't *plan* the future. Being present and staying right here, right now in this moment in time is where I'm at my best."

Is there a question that you wish someone would have asked you along the way?

"I wish more people would have asked me about the 'why,'" Jennifer says. "Why are you afraid to do that? Why are you hesitant to try that?" Had she been asked and answered these questions, she thinks she may have come to the position she is in now sooner.

Are there any quotes or thoughts that motivate you?

She says it took her a long time to understand being present in the now. When she starts to drift or obsess about the past too much or worry about the future, focusing on the present grounds her. It takes her focus to where she is now and that is what she has control over. "It doesn't mean you can't think ahead about things." She advises friends and colleagues not "to write the script before it happens. Sometimes you have to get there and not come up with what you think the result is going to be."

"If I've learned anything from losing my whole family it's that life is short. I wake up every day and say I am so glad to be alive today. I really do think this!"

Do you have any thoughts about presenting the steel industry as a viable career option to young people?

"Many young people majoring or working in communications only envision a future in the tech industry. Manufacturing and industry truly allow the world to function."

Refractories, for instance, are essential ingredients for manufacturing almost everything around us; from glass and cement to aluminum and steel. While it might not sound as sexy, there is a tremendous amount of technology in the steel industry. Technology is going to continue to drive this industry for the foreseeable future, like using digitalization to perform predictive analyses. In both manufacturing and in the steel industry you are creating something tangible. From roads, buildings, and bridges to canned food and appliances, the world is full of products made from something you have helped design and produce.

"The manufacturing and technology industries are not as divergent as some people may think."

* * *

As we wound up the interview, Jennifer shared with me something she remembered. Her mother had just returned to the workforce after raising her children and was working for a temp agency. Her first job was with the Refractory Institute. Jennifer says her mom worked with them for a long time. She remembers receiving college care packages with notes from her mother written on the institute's embossed letterhead. Today, her favorite clients are in the refractory industry. It really is a small world.

Thank you, Jennifer.

Jennifer Wylie Faines
Owner — PR Digital Communications

Jennifer Wylie Faines is a public relations and communications consultant with more than twenty-five years of experience in consumer/corporate, digital, and agency environments. As a trusted communications counselor, she develops and leads public relations, marketing communications, and social media strategic initiatives.

Clients range from manufacturing and technology companies to consumer and retail brands, health care, and cultural and nonprofit organizations. Jennifer's strategic counsel provides executive leadership and brand positioning, messaging, writing and content development, media relations, crisis communications, issues management, and brand marketing communications solutions for clients.

To learn more, visit linkedin.com/in/jenniferfaines/

CHAPTER TWELVE

Sara Dadig

Buyer

"Never underestimate the power of a hot dog."

For someone who has no background or formal training in purchasing, the idea of buying vast quantities of steel might be daunting, but not for Sara Dadig, who began her steel purchasing career two years ago when she was first hired as a purchasing assistant.

"I think purchasing is a great field for women," says Sara. "Women are good buyers. They buy most of the household goods anyway."

Sara was working in another department when the senior buyer thought she had the right personality and skills to be in purchasing. He offered her the job, and without hesitation Sara said, "Yes." She had to learn more about the basics of the steel industry, the process of buying steel, the vagaries of market fluctuations,

High school graduation

product availability, and the technicalities of negotiating contracts.

In the process, Sara discovered she was smarter
than she thought she was. She caught on quickly, and
because she has a good work ethic she is working
hard to learn as much as she can about purchasing.
One of the key components she mastered easily was
learning the importance of building relationships,
and as a result, "My favorite thing about purchasing
in general is the relationship you make with vendors," she says. "You aren't building the relationships
for when things are easy, but for when things get
tight."

Sara recognizes that steel buying may not be very
glamorous. Even though she has only been with the
company for a short time, she never expected she would
enjoy it as much as she does, and she sees a future for
herself in this field.

* * *

What are some of your challenges?

Sara says she would like to have more interaction with
management in terms of discussions around purchasing. She also thinks listening is an important skill. Her
solution is to make a concerted effort to speak up more
often and be part of the conversation.

Do you have any mentors?

Sara says her mentor is fifty-five years young and is
her best friend.

Do you see any difference between men and women in the workplace?

"Women tend to learn more than just is what is in front of them." She also thinks if you can learn every job in a department, you can fill in for someone who is absent. Also, if you want to be promoted and move up in management you can say, "I've mastered all of the jobs. I am ready for more responsibility."

Sara feels women are more detail-oriented. As a result, problems and issues are minimized or avoided, which creates a shorter path to success.

Can you think of any events that have influenced you while you have been with the company?

She admitted to meeting and falling in love with her fiancé, who also happens to work at the company. They married last summer.

Sara shared with me that the company's maintenance manager is a strong, tough guy. It was Christmas-time and she had decorated her office to look like a gingerbread house. "It looked like Christmas threw up in there," she says. He happened to stop by and commented on her decorations. She asked him if he was concerned about her office looking more festive than his area. This manager was competitive and wasn't going to be outdone. The company presented an annual award for best Christmas decorations, and after looking at Sara's office, he wanted to win it.

The maintenance manager went back to his department and created a whole North Pole theme. He had his team make metal sculptures and put lights everywhere. The maintenance department ended up winning the award that year, but Sara wanted them to know she was a Christmas force to be reckoned with. They have gone head-to-head with Christmas decorations every year since.

The last thing Sara wanted to add is that she is all about communicating and supporting employee morale. She initiated "Hot Dog Day" at the company to benefit children's charities. Management gave the plant employees extra time around lunchtime and provided hot dogs and condiments that could be purchased for one dollar. Employees gladly made additional donations and the event raised more than $600. Everyone, including executives and managers, were standing on the lawn, eating hot dogs, and talking with the hourly, production guys, many of whom they had never spoken to before. Everyone enjoyed themselves and had a great time. Afterward employees asked Sara if the company would sponsor this event more frequently.

It was a win/win event, and it only cost the company $200. Sara received such positive feedback that the event has been expanded to include chips and sodas, and donations to the local children's charities have increased. This event turned into a great way for management and the employees to get to know one another over a simple hot dog.

❆ ❆ ❆

Her advice: "Stick with it, be strong, and don't let people bully you."

And don't forget the hot dogs.

Thank you, Sara.

Acknowledgments

This book would not have been possible without women from around the world who agreed to be interviewed. Thank you for sharing your amazing stories, experiences, and thoughts. You are the inspiration behind the book, and it is your powerful stories that are fueling work on a second volume that will highlight additional women in steel. It has been a privilege to speak with you so candidly about your career paths, and how those experiences impacted your success.

Thank you to Stacy Varmecky, general manager, sales and marketing at the Association for Iron & Steel Technology (AIST), her staff, and the AIST Steering Committee for Women in Steel for supporting this idea and sending out the inquiries for the interviews. You have been instrumental in this entire process, and I look forward to working with the committee on more projects.

Appreciation goes to writer-editor Marie Lanser Beck, a Wilson College classmate and friend, who untangled the mystery of internal quotation marks and made me laugh over errors that didn't make it into print. You are a phenomenal woman, and I am so grateful for your assistance with this project.

For my friend Autumn Edmiston, who is as supportive a friend and "sister" as they come. Thank you for the phone calls, keeping me connected to the real world while I was writing, and for your ideas, thoughts, dinners, and supplying copious amounts of chocolate when needed. I am grateful you are on this journey with me and that you like chocolate too.

Thank you to David Aretha, my editor, who was responsive, supportive, and flexible with my edits and submission process. It was great to work with you!

To my friend Mary Ann Merriman, whom I met at a networking event five years ago. We have been friends since we learned that we were both in the steel industry during a time when there were very few women working in the field. I love our conversations, brainstorming sessions, and talking about our steel experiences. Thank you, my friend, for reminding me to take care of myself through this process.

To Maggie McLaughlin, who is extremely patient and great at organizing everything into book form. She describes herself as Amazing, Fantastic, and a Resourceful Woman Who Does Everything. Thank you, Maggie.

To Christy Day from Constellation Book Services, thank you for a creative and strong cover that reflects the talented women I have interviewed.

For my mentors, customers, and colleagues along the way. Thank you for the opportunity to have worked with you and learn from you. It has been an incredible ride and I have the stories to prove it.

To the steel industry. How many industries in today's work environment do we hear the word "family" mentioned? I heard the word "brothers" and "sisters" often in my interviews. In this world where so many people are looking for a place to belong, you can become part of a family in the steel industry.

My respect is beyond measure for the men and

women in this industry who work on the the mill floors and in the melt shops, pulpits, cranes, labs, IT, shipping, production, and quality control as well as all the administrative, sales, and management staff that make this industry happen every single day.

> **"How good it is for us to recognize and celebrate our heroes and she-roes!**
> *– Maya Angelou*

With Compassion,

Karin J. Lund

About the Author

Karin J. Lund was one of the first women in North America to be hired by a major integrated steel mill for an outside sales position. Jones & Laughlin Steel (J&L Steel) head-quartered in Pittsburgh, Pa., which would later become LTV, offered her a sales position following her graduation from Wilson College in 1976. As part of a two-year training program, she spent twelve months in the Pittsburgh sales office where she also served as J&L's corporate United Way representative.

In 1978 Lund was assigned to J&L's Cincinnati, Ohio office and in February 1979 she was recruited by a Canadian steel company, Co-Steel, headquartered in Whitby, Ontario. At the time the company owned Lake Ontario Steel Company (LASCO) in Whitby, and Chaparral Steel in Midlothian, Texas.

Co-Steel wanted to expand its operations in the American market and built a new state-of-the-art electric furnace melt shop and wire rod mill in Perth Amboy, New Jersey. At the time, the electric arc furnace was the highest-powered electric furnace in the world. She joined the company, Raritan River Steel, while the company was still in the early construction stages of building the new mill. As a product specialist Lund was tasked with organizing an order entry system for sales which interfaced with every department throughout the mill including shipping and invoicing. While in Perth Amboy, Lund was involved in sales and sales training, conducted mill tours for customers and visitors including a group behind President Jimmy Carter, and organized the company's participation at industry conventions.

Lund was on the road again early in 1982 and was later promoted to central regional sales manager. She managed an international sales territory with annual sales of $140 million and at one time managed ten of the company's top twenty-five accounts. She was the first of her colleagues to successfully call on and conduct business with the competition. At the request of legal counsel, she testified twice before the International Trade Commission on anti-dumping trade cases. She represented the company at the Cold Finished Steel Bar Institute meetings and regularly met with politicians while in Washington, DC for those meetings. She also received three Certificates of Outstanding Service from the American Iron and Steel Institute (AISI) through the Steel Fellows Program for encouraging college graduates, particularly women, to join the steel industry. She was even included – a lone woman-in a photograph in Life magazine with approximately twenty male managers at the mill shortly after it was built.

Lund was with customers at the mill, which was forty-five minutes from New York City on 9/11, and immediately volunteered at the American Red Cross in South Jersey and organized a fundraiser benefitting the local chapter. In the aftermath of Hurricane Katrina, she organized a small group of volunteers and adopted a Catholic grade school with 250 students in

Bay St. Louis, Mississippi which had been decimated by the storm. With overwhelming support from her customers both in the United States and Canada, Lund and her group raised more than $30,000 in donations, food, and gifts for the children, teachers, and families at the school and sponsored a Christmas dinner for 850 people. The group helped with construction and repair of homes and fed over 1,200 people during their visit.

Lund left the industry in 2006, several years after Co-Steel Raritan was purchased by Gerdau-Ameristeel.

About G-Power Global Enterprises

Lund is the founder of G-Power Global Enterprises and an Amazon bestselling author of *Compassion is the Competitive Edge-Leading with Compassion while Delivering Results*. She also wrote *The Language of Loss-Breaking the Silence-Starting Conversations about Loss at Work and Home*. Volume II of *Women in Steel, Women Of Steel-Yesterday, Today & Tomorrow* will be available in May 2023.

Her online program, *Your Journey through the Islands of Life and Loss,* is an experiential and interactive program for employers that helps employees, individually confront issues related to their own personal journeys around change, life events and loss.

G-Power is focused on bringing employees and management together around a compassionate culture in the workplace. When companies lead with compassion, they will inherently create a competitive market advantage which drives productivity and profits.

Lund is available for speaking and consulting.

For more information visit her website at G-Power-Global.com or email her at Sales@G-PowerGlobal.com

G-Power
SERIES

Compassion
is the
Competitive
Edge

Leading with Compassion while Delivering Results

Karin J. Lund

G-Power
GLOBAL

Your Journey
Through
the
Islands
of
Life and Loss

Karin J. Lund

G-Power
SERIES

The
Language
of Loss

Breaking the Silence –
Starting Conversations at
Work and Home

Karin J. Lund

WOMEN IN STEEL

WOMEN OF STEEL

Yesterday, Today & Tomorrow

Volume II

Karin J. Lund

MAY 2023